THE GOLF SECRET

Some opinions of *The Golf Secret*

Records Broken in Praise . . .

ELIXIR OF GOLFING LIFE . . .
EVERY SHOT DOWN THE MIDDLE

Sir William Hunt writes
'Read The Golf Secret . . . at once straighter and longer shots . . . if I
follow your teaching, a good shot inevitable . . . found elixir of golfing
life . . . have just won Founders' foursomes, thanks to your book . . .
every shot down the middle . . .'

FOUND THE SECRET AT 85 YEARS

**Mr. George P. Bancroft, Elibank House, Taplow, Bucks., in an unsolicited
letter, writes**
'I am nearing 85 . . . have been struggling to find the golf secret for fifty
years . . . different man since reading your wonderful book and practising
its instruction . . .'

PAST PRESIDENT OF THE ENGLISH GOLF
UNION, WRITES

**Mr. George Henriques, a past President of the English Golf Union and
International golfer, writes**
'It is excellent and you have really hit the nail on the head,' referring to
The Golf Secret.

DID HOLE IN ONE, WON COMPETITION

Arthur Shorter, Esq., 43b, Blackwater Rd., Eastbourne, Sussex
'. . . Did hole in one . . . won first competition since 1936 . . . then won
monthly spoon with 67 net . . . handicap down.'

THE GOLF SECRET

by
H. A. MURRAY M.D.

Preface by
ALGY EASTERBROOK

PAPERFRONTS
ELLIOT RIGHT WAY BOOKS
KINGSWOOD SURREY UK

Set, printed and bound in Great Britain by
Cox & Wyman Ltd, Reading

*This book is dedicated to the memory of
my great friend the late
ISADORE SAMUELS
who first aroused my interest in Golf*

CONTENTS

DIAGRAMS

FOREWORD
to the 1st Edition

HAVING been for thirty-two years a golf professional, I did not think I could learn anything from a golf book, but having read *The Golf Secret*, I have to confess that I have learnt a great deal.

I have known Dr. Murray for many years, and known of his analytical approach to golf, so that when he asked me to consider writing the 'Preface' to his book, I felt sure it would be interesting if nothing more. It is much more!

He has apparently shown us professionals what we do and how we do it, by proving what happens to us all during the course of the swing; even though we ourselves hold many divergent views on this subject.

I have read many golf books which purported to show the easy way to play golf, and for years have endeavoured to teach the game in the simplest way, but I have never seen the golf swing described, or thought of it, in so simple and straightforward a manner as in this book.

The Author has carefully analysed the golf swing, and the factors which put it into a groove, thus simplifying its cultivation. He also appears to have proved that most of the movements of the golf swing (so interminably described and contradicted in other books), occur automatically and subconsciously.

I do honestly think he has *hit the nail on the head*. It will certainly be easier to learn by his methods.

By following the principles suggested in this book, I believe that the ordinary golfer will acquire a reliable swing that will stand him in good stead, better than the swings described by many leading players, which are based on what each of them believes to be his own particular game.

It is my considered opinion that every golfer should read

this book. The amount of information it contains is incredible. The anatomical information, as applied to golf – which I am sure has never before been published – is worth the price of the book. It explains much that we did not fully understand, and shows golf from an entirely new angle.

I feel sure that none will read *The Golf Secret* without improvement in their playing and knowledge of the game.

Dr. Murray has done a great service to the game of golf, and to all golfers. I congratulate him. I do not need to wish this book success – that is inevitable.

ALGY EASTERBROOK

AUTHOR'S PREFACE TO 4TH EDITION

I wish to emphasize one small but important fact about the backswing that will make all the difference between success and failure.

By watching any of them play, or studying their 'action photographs', my readers can confirm, as I have done, that they all hold the left shoulder high at address, and that it is *very* high at impact, proving that it *must* have gone upwards.

Now since, in any form of hitting, all bodily movements must be synchronized and in the *same direction*, that is further proof of my contention that the feeling of the forward swing is one of hitting upwards.

This is best achieved by starting the forward swing with an upward movement of the left shoulder, which will ensure an inside-to-out *grooved* swing.

When that happy state is reached the golfer can get extra length by hitting upwards with the *right* arm. (See context.)

Incidentally, experts such as Henry Cotton, who claim that the forward swing is entirely a right handed affair, must hit upwards, thus *pushing* the left shoulder upwards.

Hitting upwards ensures an inside-to-out grooved swing, fastest club head speed at and after impact, a full follow through, and a long straight shot.

Don't let any expert convince you that this is 'scooping', because even though the correct feeling is of hitting upwards, the *club head* (except in the case of the Driver with the ball tee-d up and well forward) contacts the ball at the bottom of the arc as it is descending.

So, *hit upwards*, and bring your handicap downwards!

AUTHOR

INTRODUCTION

GOLF, as played by the leading professionals of today, is played the correct way, but they have, as a body, failed to tell would-be golfers how to do it. Why? Presumably because they 'know not what they do'. Subsequently, I quote twelve leading players on starting the backswing, and twelve on the forward swing. In each instance they give twelve different versions. Since these two movements are universally admitted to be the very essence of golf, there can be no doubt about the truth of my indictment.

What chance has the unfortunate pupil-golfer of succeeding? Maybe he takes a lesson, or six lessons, or a dozen. He swings, and swings, and swings, until his hands are sore and blistered – which is often due to the loose grip he has been told to use. Still the ball won't go straight, so he reads another book, which probably makes matters worse, because he tries to copy the intermediate positions depicted in the photographs. I have discovered that these intermediate positions – such as the middle of the backswing – are not voluntarily 'gone into'. To deliberately swing into them will always produce a faulty swing. More of that later.

Our learner will then probably accept a tip from a friend (or from a professional, as I have done on many occasions), which, at the time, appears to help him. But soon another fault appears, requiring further advice.

So it goes on, month after month, year after year, always patching and tinkering.

Regarding golf books – not to mention magazine and newspaper articles – I think during the last eighteen years I must have read almost every one that has been published, and tried all the many methods therein advocated. Although latterly I have lost faith in golf books. I must admit that I have learnt a lot from them, but chiefly from *really* studying the photographs, and finding there much that was not pointed out by the authors. Many of these books are full of beautiful photographs with captions purporting to describe what has taken place, but rarely explaining how it happened or was done. For example, I have often read such statements as – 'You can see the left hand is in control', 'You can see the light right hand grip', 'You can see I am hitting downwards', 'You can see all the weight is on the right (or left) leg'. I could go on indefinitely, but the point is that neither I nor anyone else can see any of those things. In fact sometimes I think I can see just the opposite. The truth is that the writer is often 'seeing' in the photographs what he does, or even more likely, what he thinks he does. Golf literature is notoriously contradictory!

It has been said that only twenty per cent of all who play golf can go round in less than ninety, and that only that twenty per cent are entitled to call themselves golfers. Just imagine! Eighty out of every hundred who play golf are 'rabbits'. I hope they will all buy this book, and graduate to the other category.

There must be some reason for so much bad golf, and intelligent people's inability to knock a stationary ball in a straight line. It is not lack of enthusiasm, as every golfer – and his wife – knows.

There must be *something* that all professionals do, which they are unable to pass on.

Although there are slight differences, and maybe peculiarities, in professionals' set-up and action, they all swing, basically, the same way. Presumably this is the much talked-of grooved swing. But how is it done? The answer to that, my studies, experiments and observations have provided.

There are lots of 'theories' about golf, but hitherto there has been no real, universal, acceptable 'golf theory'. Nothing, as there is in other professions, that you could set about learning with the certainty that it was right, and would work. Producing just that was the task which I set myself. Let me emphasize that that did not entail discovering a new method of playing golf, but merely finding out what the professionals do, and how they do it: avoiding the idiosyncrasies and eccentricities, and finding the 'common denominator'.

That is what I claim to have done.

During my investigations, I have come to the conclusion that all professionals are right in some of the things they teach, but none of them know all the answers. For example, some are right in demanding a firm or very firm grip; others are right in allowing the head to *turn* soon after impact; and others are right in stressing the importance of a ninety degree shoulder turn on the backswing when playing a full shot. Others, who disagree with these precepts – in my view – are wrong.

Most of my contentions are supported by someone in authority, or by some detail in their photographs. I have deliberately avoided the use of photographs because I am sure that they lead most people astray in trying to assume the sequence of positions portrayed, which are really quite incidental to a correctly executed swing. Instead, I have drawn several diagrams which more precisely show one's meaning.

I would like to acknowledge my indebtedness to Algy Easterbrook for many inspirations, and also for consenting to write the 'Foreword' – 'if the manuscript proved acceptable to him'.

After reading this book you will be able – in less weeks than it took me years – to 'swing in the groove', and knock the ball straight and far, quite easily, with certainty, and without the many 'do's' and 'don'ts' normally required. You will be able to by-pass the many mistakes which I have made – and practised – during many years, but you will also be deprived of the pleasure of profiting by your mistakes. Perhaps you would prefer to profit by mine!

A NOTE FROM THE PUBLISHER

SINCE the late Dr. Murray wrote 'The Golf Secret' in 1956, there have been many changes among the personalities on the golf scene, but 'The Golf Secret' will always stand the test of time.

With the passage of years, many of the famous golfers mentioned in this book have passed the height of their powers, and new 'greats' appear annually on our television screens in the competitions of the giants. So, it may be that younger readers will know little of Henry Cotton, Harry Varden, George Duncan, Bobby Jones and others mentioned in these pages. Perhaps each reader should substitute his own current idols for these names, because it is certain that the winners of major championships in the last quarter of the 20th Century know and possess 'The Golf Secret' just like those of earlier years.

'The Golf Secret' has had, and continues to have, an enormous influence on players and professionals – indeed it has sold over 150,000 copies in the English language since first published. With this in mind I have decided not to try to amend Dr. Murray's work by up-dating the names of famous players that he mentioned – I leave it as Dr. Murray wrote it and publish this third impression of the sixth edition, certain that it will remain 'the golfers' bible'.

No matter how much fashions and personalities may alter, 'The Golf Secret' remains eternal.

A. G. ELLIOT

DIAGRAM No. 1 – CLUB LOFTS AND DISTANCES
Arrows Represent Flight of Ball, at Right Angles to Club Face

APPROX. LOFT IN DEGREES		
WOODS		
YARDS (AVERAGE)		
IRONS		
APPROX. LOFT IN DEGREES		

Woods:

No.	1	2	3	4
Approx. loft in degrees	10	13	22	25
Yards (average)	200	190	180	170

Irons:

No.	1	2	3	4	5	6	7	8	9
Yards (average)	170	160	150	140	130	120	110	100	90
Approx. loft in degrees	20	23	25	30	35	40	45	48	50

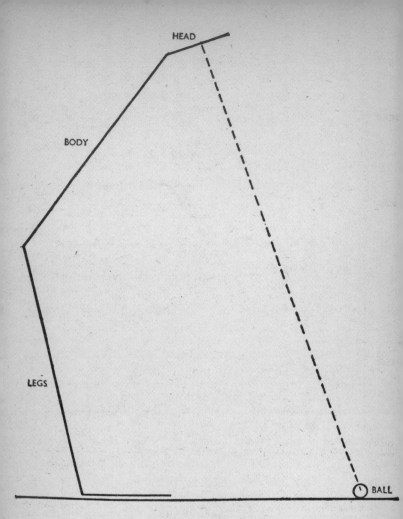

DIAGRAM No. 2 – FACE THE BALL

Don't look down your nose at the ball. At the address, your eyes should be wide open, which they can be only if your face faces downwards to the ball. Remember that the ball is on the ground, and not in the air – that is, under you, rather than in front of you. Your face and chest will then be approximately at right angles to a line connecting them to the ball.

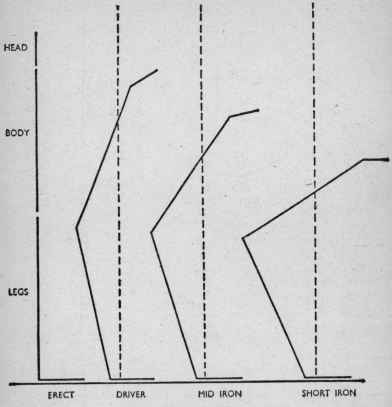

HEAD

BODY

LEGS

ERECT   DRIVER   MID IRON   SHORT IRON

DIAGRAM No. 3.– BACK BENDING

DOTTED LINE = CENTRE OF GRAVITY

Note the relative positions of head and buttocks when using clubs of different lengths.
With any golf stroke the body is far from the normal erect standing position; and as the
club becomes shorter, the head and shoulders go forwards and downwards, while the
buttocks go backwards. Thus you maintain your centre of gravity, and consequently,
your balance.

LONG CLUBS   MEDIUM CLUBS   SHORT CLUBS

DIAGRAM No. 4 – SILHOUETTES OF EXPERTS

Note, from behind the shot, *firstly*, the resemblance (with any club) of the body shape to a 'reversed question mark'; and becoming more so with shorter clubs; *secondly*, the practically horizontal upper part of the spine; *thirdly*, the practically perpendicular arms (represented by the arrows). With slight variations of this leg and back bending, photographs of most experts conform to this diagram. If you have to stand more upright than this, your clubs are too long. Shorten them.

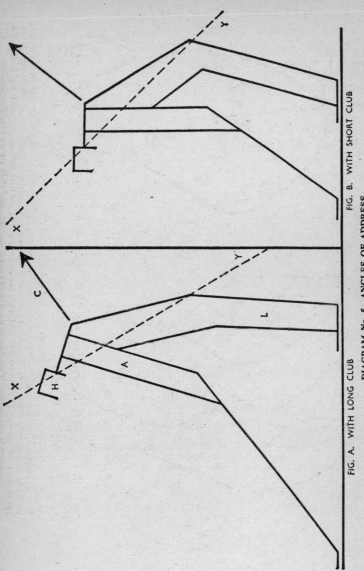

FIG. A. WITH LONG CLUB   FIG. B. WITH SHORT CLUB

DIAGRAM No. 5 – ANGLES OF ADDRESS

L – The Legs. A – The Arms. H – The Head. C – The Club. XY – The 'Entire Spine'

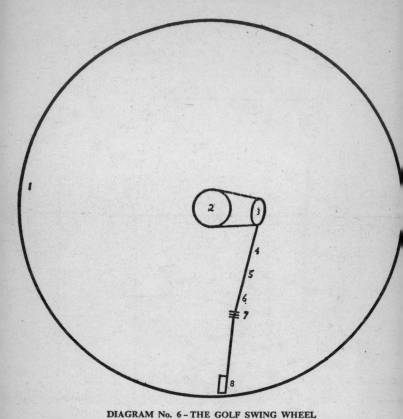

DIAGRAM No. 6 – THE GOLF SWING WHEEL

1 – RIM OF WHEEL, OR PATH OF CLUB HEAD.   2 – HUB OF WHEEL, OR HUB OF THE SWING,
i.e. UPPER SPINE.   3 – LEFT SHOULDER.   4 – UPPER ARM.   5 – ELBOW.   6 – FOREARM.
7 – HAND, GRIPPING CLUB.   8 – CLUB HEAD.   2 to 8 – SPOKE OF WHEEL

FIG. A. ADDRESS   FIG. B. BACKSWING BEGUN

DIAGRAM No. 7 – THE FLATTENED ARC

1 – HORIZONTAL UPPER SPINE. 2 – LEFT SHOULDER. 3 – RIGHT SHOULDER. 4 – LEFT ARM. 5 – RIGHT ARM. 6 – HANDS. 7 – CLUB. 8 – BALL. 9 – CURVED ARC. 10 – FLATTENED ARC

A. SHOULDER LINE SOON AFTER IMPACT –
OBSERVER FACING THE PLAYER, SHOUL-
DERS 45 DEGREES TO PERPENDICULAR.
1 – LEFT SHOULDER.
2 – RIGHT SHOULDER.

B. SHOULDER LINE SOON AFTER IMPACT.
OBSERVER TO RIGHT OF PLAYER, BEHIND
THE SHOT. SHOULDERS 30 DEGREES, OR
LESS, TO PERPENDICULAR
1 – LEFT SHOULDER.
2 – RIGHT SHOULDER.

DIAGRAM No. 8 – THE SHOULDER ANGLES

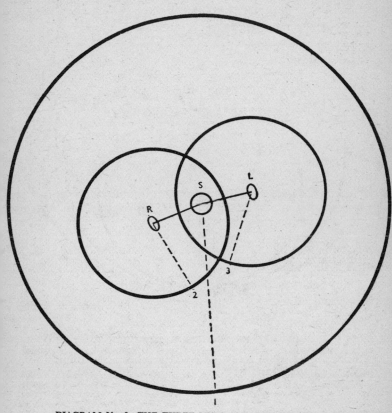

DIAGRAM No. 9 – THE THREE HUBS AND THE THREE ARCS

S – Spine. R – Right Shoulder. L – Left Shoulder. 1 – Spine Arc. 2 – Right
Shoulder Arc. 3 – Left Shoulder Arc

The right shoulder joint is the axis of the right arm swing, the left shoulder joint the axis
of the left arm swing, but the spine is the central axis of the main, or body, swing. Thus
both shoulders (i.e. the body) and the arms, hands, and the club, 'attached' to them, are
merely revolved around the horizontal upper part of the spine. The arm-swings may be
assisted voluntarily, but centrifugal force is the main factor in synchronizing the 'three
swings', with consequent good timing.

SHOULDER

ELBOW

WRIST

CLUB

DIAGRAM No. 10 – THE SHOULDER SWING

1 – CLUB ONLY, NARROW SWING.   2 – FOREARM AND CLUB, MEDIUM SWING.   3 – WHOLE ARM AND CLUB, WIDE SWING

When studying the arm swing alone, it should be noted that a swing started by the hand must voluntarily bend the wrist, and consequently be narrow. The desirable wide swing is produced by swinging the arm from its 'top end' by means of the shoulder muscles. This applies to the left arm on the backswing and the right arm on the forward swing. Your hands should merely firmly grip the club shaft, thereby becoming 'part of it'. Centrifugal force will automatically cock and uncock your wrists. All wrist action should be automatic and involuntary.

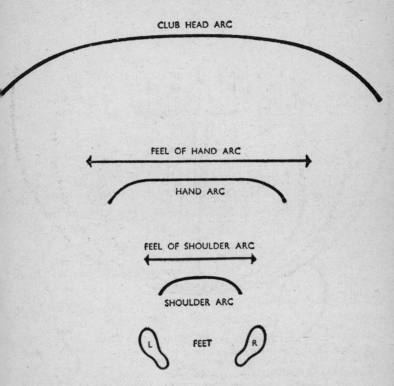

CLUB HEAD ARC

FEEL OF HAND ARC

HAND ARC

FEEL OF SHOULDER ARC

SHOULDER ARC

L   FEET   R

DIAGRAM No. 11 – THE ARCS – OVERHEAD VIEW

BALL

IMPACT

CLUB HEAD

FS

HANDS

L R   L R

FEET

L   R

DIAGRAM No. 12 – FASTEST CLUB HEAD SPEED
F.S. – REGION OF FASTEST CLUB HEAD SPEED

DIAGRAM No. 13 – DIVOTS

A divot is the earth removed by the club head, after impact with the ball if intentional, before impact if unintentional. In the diagram, the line connecting the letters A to F to ball, represents arms and club. (A) Hands above ball; no divot. (B) Hands ahead of ball; small divot. (C) Hands farther ahead of ball; large divot. (D) Hands above, but too near the ball (many reasons); unintentional divot. (E) Weight too far to right at impact; unintentional divot, followed by topped ball. (F) Hands ahead of ball to extract partly submerged ball; two intentional divots, small one before, and large one after, impact.

Are divots necessary? Harry Vardon didn't think so. George Duncan doesn't. Therefore I am in good company! See text; for and against.

DIAGRAM No. 14 – BACK SPIN

Backspin! The inevitable spin with which a golf ball travels when struck with any club except a straightfaced putter, provided no tee is used and ball is not topped. It is therefore unnecessary to make any effort to apply backspin. In the diagram, (A) represents No. 9 iron striking ball with no divot. (B) No. 9 converted to No. 7, ball farther to the right with intention of taking a divot. (C) No. 9 converted to No. 5, ball still farther to the right with intention of taking larger divot. Where is the advantage of the divot-taking blows over the other, for, as the diagram shows, all three are tangents to a circle and must produce equal backspin? In fact, the advantage of the no divot blow, which at impact will be more directly towards the target, should be a greater forward propulsion – the primary object!

Chapter 1

THE GOLF SECRET – FIRST FACTOR

Shape of the Body.
Length of Club Shaft.
Body Movements.
Angles of Address.
Function of Spine.
Upright and Flat Swings.
The Feel of the Golf Swing.
The Correct Attitude.

Shape of the Body

The first thing to realize when playing golf is that the ball to be hit is on the ground. This is not such a stupid observation as it may seem. I have watched hundreds of golfers who apparently don't realize it, or at any rate do not appreciate the importance of bending their bodies to 'face the ball'. They stand almost erect with arms stuck forward, looking down their noses at the ball – the attitude in which they could best strike a ball off a post a few feet above the ground.

Visualize yourself hitting a ball chest high on the face of a wall. You would not lie on your back but would stand erect; i.e. you would face the ball. Now visualize the ball on the ground (the plane of which is of course ninety degrees to the wall) and you will see why you should not stand erect when playing golf, but should bend your back, i.e. you should face the ball.

The ball must be looked at with wide open eyes. Address a ball, then stand erect with your eyes wide open and looking straight ahead. Now without glancing down at the ball, bend

29

the upper part of your body forward until the ball comes into your line of vision. Your face and chest will now be approximately at right angles to a line connecting them to the ball – as they should be. See diagram No. 2. You will probably now be too near the ball.

In diagram No. 3, the diagrammatic angles serve to give an idea of the relative positions of the head and buttocks when using different length clubs. The farther the head goes down the farther it will go forward, and consequently the farther must the buttocks go backwards to maintain your centre of gravity and, consequently, your balance. That is why, at the address position, an expert golfer's trousers (being stretched over the protruding buttocks), hang straight down at the back and cling to the front of the thighs.

Broadly speaking, the body assumes the shape of a 'reversed question mark' (see diagram No. 4). The drawings in this diagram are not copied from photographs of any one player. They are composite drawings showing approximately the shape of the backs – and spines – of most of the world's best golfers. The reader can confirm this by studying photographs in many golf books.

There are individual variations of back and leg bending, but they mostly conform, more or less, to our diagram No. 4.

When studying the leg bending the reader should remember that the actual shape of the legs is somewhat camouflaged by the straight-hanging back of the trousers.

The feature which I wish to stress, is that with all these players, and with all lengths of clubs, the upper part of the spine, i.e. that between the shoulders, is approximately horizontal (parallel to the ground).

This portion of the spine is prolonged by a 'dotted line' in diagram No. 4, to show more clearly how it approaches, or even exceeds, the horizontal.

The arrows indicate the angle of the arms, which in all cases is approximately at right angles to the upper part of the spine.

It is this shape of the body that ensures the hands coming

straight down on the forward swing, and consequently maintaining the angle between the arm and the club shaft, and compelling the club head to get to ground level behind the ball. Without this spine bending you would tend to swing over the ball or to top it.

I think a series of photographs showing a sequence of positions through the golf swing is harmful, because the reader will endeavour to swing into these various positions, and will consequently swing in the wrong manner or in the wrong direction.

The positions to study are those from 'behind the shot' when the player is at the address position; and a little before impact (before the left shoulder has risen too high), when the almost, or actually, horizontal upper part of the spine will be best seen.

The first eight inches or so below the neck, which 'connects' the two shoulders is the vital part of the spine in golf.

In photographs, as in the diagram, it will be seen that with all clubs, this part of the back, and therefore spine, is approximately parallel to the ground, at the address and just before impact.

Also obvious in experts' photographs is the arm position. At the address and just before impact it is virtually at right angles to the upper part of the spine. Therefore the arms hang down vertically, except maybe with the longer clubs when the hands may be just a little farther forward.

LENGTH OF CLUB SHAFT

Intimately connected with back-bending is the subject of length of club shaft.

I am certain that many people would play better golf if they shortened their club shafts. Most average golfers play short shots better than long ones. With short clubs they have to bend their backs.

Many handicap golfers prefer the mashie to the driver, and

often get as far with it. Again many players cannot use the number two.

Professionals know that these facts are indisputable.

The difficulty is due to the length of shaft necessitating the player standing too erect. When I made this discovery I had my long clubs shortened with immediate and marked benefit. Theoretically, the club head should travel faster at impact with a longer shaft; in practice, if the club does not 'fit' the player, it does not.

Again, many of the modern 'short-backswing professionals' claim to drive as far as they can with the longer backswing, even though the club head has a shorter journey to impact, just as it has when the club is shorter.

Even if we admit that there might be a slight loss of length, is it not better to have reasonable length 'down the middle' every time, than an occasional one that goes a few yards farther?

Before having your shafts shortened, experiment by putting a rubber band on all long shafts, placing the band at the length of your favourite club, then grip below it. The bit of shaft above your left hand may worry you, but I think the result will surprise you.

If the shortened shafts necessitate an alteration of the 'lie', it is a simple matter with the irons. During my many experiments I had my irons 'acetylene-blowlamped', and bent at the neck on two occasions by a local engineering firm. The woods might need new heads. Actually, however, the shaft shortening will not usually call for alteration of the lie, because if the club head was flat on the ground when you were standing too erect, then when you make the upper part of your spine horizontal, your hands will go down and the toe of the club head will come up; but when you shorten the club shaft the club head will come nearer to you and will again – usually – be flat on the ground.

I am not suggesting that all clubs should be the same length, but even that might be worth considering, since most of the difference in distance, with different clubs, is due to the degree of loft.

The slight distance advantage possible by using varying lengths of shaft, is more than outweighed by the difficulties they create, at any rate in the case of high and medium handicap players. With longer shafts there is a gradual pushing forward of hands and the body is less bent with a consequent flattening of the swing.

I think that most readers will now be persuaded to experiment with shorter shafts.

Before leaving this subject of back-bending and clubs 'to fit' the player, I will mention another relevant fact. Observant golfers must have noticed that many professionals have 'round shoulders'. This is because their backs are constantly bent during play, so that ultimately the upper part of their spines become permanently nearer the horizontal than the vertical. It could well be termed an 'occupational deformity', as some of them walk about with the upper part of their bodies in something approaching the address position or 'set'.

Remember, a crouching attitude is necessary to hit a ball on the ground.

BODY MOVEMENTS

It is necessary to have a clear mental picture of the golf swing, particularly as it affects the player's body. Then, the same body movements can be made every time, instead of the mind being full of many possible ways of hitting the ball, each method fighting for supremacy.

The mental picture is of the shoulders revolving around the upper part of the spine, at right angles to its axis, a quarter of a circle on the backswing and half a circle on the forward swing.

This at once implies the body acting before, and doing more than, the arms.

This mental picture is so important that it will bear amplification so that it will be impressed on the reader's mind, never to be forgotten. I will call it the GOLDEN RULE:

THE CONSCIOUS PART OF ANY GOLF SWING, BACK AND FOR-

WARD, IS ESSENTIALLY A PERPENDICULAR TURNING OF THE SHOULDERS AROUND A HORIZONTAL UPPER PART OF THE SPINE.

That is all you do, consciously.

All other movements which occur below the level of the armpits – including those of the hips, legs, and feet – during the course of the golf swing, are secondary, compensatory, subconscious, and occur automatically, without any assistance from the player.

ANGLES OF ADDRESS

I will now clarify diagram No. 5 which I have called 'Angles of Address'.

In each of the figures of this diagram there are three vertical planes, two right-angles, and one obtuse angle.

(1) The three vertical planes are the legs, the arms (including the shoulders), and the head. The arms and shoulders are farther forward than the legs, and the head is farther forward than the arms. Think of these three planes as being relatively parallel.

(2) The two right-angles are that formed by the arms and the upper part of the spine and that formed by the club shaft at address and an imaginary line passing through the top and bottom ends of the entire spine.

This imaginary line (the dotted line in the diagram), may be taken as representing the line of the entire spine. Therefore the sum of the twists around the upper and lower portions of the spine will cause the club shaft, when nearing the top of the backswing, to be at right-angles to this imaginary line (as it was at the address), and therefore pointing backwards and to the sky in line with the club shaft at address, just as though the club had revolved around that line. But, I must make it clear that the club is definitely *not swung* around that line, as the reader will soon learn.

(3) The obtuse angle is formed at the left wrist, by the arms and the club shaft.

It will be noted in the diagram that, when playing with the shorter club, the buttocks go backwards making the legs less perpendicular, and the head and shoulders go forward and down, making the upper part of the spine more horizontal. Consequently the hands come backwards, causing the arms to be more perpendicular and thus maintaining the right angle between them and the upper part of the spine, so reducing the obtuse angle between them and the club shaft.

The right-angle between the club shaft and the imaginary line through the ends of the spine is maintained, both at the address and when approaching the top of the backswing.

Owing to these changes – particularly the greater degree of back bending – the swing will be more upright.

FUNCTION OF SPINE

Before proceeding to a detailed study of the action of the spine in executing the golf swing, it will be well to have some understanding of its elementary anatomy and function.

The spine consists of a number of separate segments, called vertebrae, which may be likened to a string of large square beads. Imagine the string being pulled very tight. Then, as with the spine, a little movement would be possible in all directions, including a slight twist.

Apart from your ability to bend forward, that twist is the important movement in the golf swing. Now for details.

In the neck there are seven 'cervical' vertebrae.

In the chest there are twelve 'costal' vertebrae, so called because the ribs are attached to them.

Between the ribs and the hip bones there are five 'lumbar' vertebrae; and below these there is the fixed portion of the spine, i.e. the 'sacrum' – by means of which the spine is attached to the 'pelvis' or hip bones.

Let us see to what extent it is possible to twist the spine.

The cervical spine, i.e. the portion in the neck, will twist approximately seventy degrees, while the remainder – i.e. the combined costal and lumbar spine – will twist approximately forty-five degrees only.

Stand sideways to a mirror, and turn your head to look into it. This will prove that about seventy degrees is the maximum turn in the 'neck spine' (that is, of the head) in most people, without moving the shoulders.

Now, keep turning your head until your face is square to the mirror and you will find that your shoulder must go back to some extent.

Incidentally, that demonstrates the desirability of, or at least the reason for, turning the head to the right when addressing the ball. It permits a full 'shoulder-pivot' of ninety degrees.

A lot of famous players don't turn their heads to the right at address; instead they must allow their heads to be turned to the right during the course of the backswing by the full shoulder pivot.

With lesser players, who are so determined to keep their heads still that they thereby prevent a full shoulder turn, it is definitely preferable to turn the head at address.

Each person should find out into which of these categories he comes, then adopt the method which suits him.

Personally, I prefer to look straight at the ball in a natural manner, and to allow the head to be turned, both on the backswing and the forward swing, by the shoulders.

By swinging, as I will later describe, your head will turn naturally, and you need not worry about 'head up'.

Now, to continue the study of the spine twist, stand erect, this time facing a mirror, and twist your shoulders ninety degrees to the right into the position they should be at the top of the backswing.

You will find that your hips have turned (by their own volition, and without your help, or even knowledge), approximately half as far as your shoulders, i.e. forty-five degrees.

Therefore the difference between the hip and shoulder turns (forty-five degrees), represents the maximum amount of twist possible in the combined costal and lumbar spines; i.e. – for our purpose – the entire spine.

In many older people the spine will not twist to that extent, therefore if they wish to play worth-while golf, they will have to choose between two methods of playing a full shot – both imperfect.

(1) A full shoulder pivot with almost as much hip pivot, which will compel the left heel to come too far off the ground.

(2) A part shoulder pivot with a normal hip pivot, which will leave the heel down, but will shorten the back swing. This will usually be the better method.

Therefore before again attempting the impossible on a golf course, see what you are capable of in a mirror. Bearing in mind the shape of the spine as a whole when correctly addressing the ball (see diagrams Nos. 4 and 5), we will trace what happens to it during the course of the golf swing, briefly indicating what happens to other parts of the body in consequence.

On the backswing, the horizontal upper part of the spine is twisted on its axis to the right. This carries the arms, hands, and club straight to the right, while the left shoulder goes down and the right shoulder goes up; and both hips move slightly to the right. Very soon that upper part of the spine is tightly twisted, then the lower more vertical part of the spine also twists to the right. This carries the shoulders, arms, hands and club somewhat around you, i.e. 'inside the line'. The entire spine is now screwed tightly to the right and that happens soon, since a twist of only forty-five degrees is possible.

To continue the backswing, something else must 'give'. The twisted spine pulls the left hip forwards and pushes the right hip backwards, which carries the shoulders, arms, hands and club still farther around you. Meanwhile, the left shoulder goes farther down and the right shoulder farther up.

On the forward swing this winding-up is undone progressively, and then wound-up to the left, the process beginning subconsciously in the lower more vertical part of the spine.

During the first small portion of the voluntary unwinding of the upper part of the spine, there is a greater (though automatic) unwinding of the more vertical lower part of the spine, resulting in a backward movement of the left hip. (This fact, which will be better understood after reading Chapter 2, causes many players, including some experts, to think the forward swing is begun with the left hip.)

As the lower more vertical part of the spine continues to wind to the left, the winding process is passed upwards to the horizontal upper part of the spine, which in turn finally becomes completely wound to the left – after impact. At this stage, since the spine twisting is complete the right hip is pulled farther forwards by the impetus of the swing.

UPRIGHT AND FLAT SWINGS

It is often said that an open stance causes an upright swing. I think not. The left foot being farther back, in effect 'shortens' the left leg, which naturally tends to check the automatic hip turn to the right. If this occurs it gives the *appearance* of an upright swing. With the same degree of back bending the swing can be upright or flat only if the swing itself varies, i.e. if in some instances the swing is wrongly executed. For example, using the hands to hold the face shut on the backswing, or swaying, will tend to produce an exaggerated upright swing; while deliberately opening the club face on the backswing by a wrist roll and/or swinging the club round the right leg will produce a flat swing.

These are wrong methods necessitating different swings for different shots.

A true flat or upright swing depends on the degree of erectness or bending of the body. Providing the swing is always the same (which it should be unless you prefer to complicate the game), then the more erect the body the flatter the swing will be, and the more bent the body the more upright.

That is why, with a shorter club shaft, the swing automatically becomes more upright. And why a tall player, who must bend to reach the ball, almost invariably swings upright; while the short player – if he uses clubs of average length which will be too long for him – must stand more erect and usually swing flat.

THE FEEL OF THE GOLF SWING

I am going to describe what I believe to be a unique method of acquiring the 'feel' of the golf swing.

Grip a golf club, then stand perfectly upright with arms reasonably outstretched in front of you. Your hands should be about level with the middle of your 'tummy', shoulders forward and upper arms lightly touching your chest. The club shaft will be horizontal, i.e. parallel to the floor.

Now swing the club straight round to the right, then straight round to the left, so that you feel that your hands and the club are travelling in a 'straight' line, by which I mean all the time on the same plane, parallel to the floor.

Repeat several times until you get some freedom, then swing to the right, stop, and look. Actually the hands have gone a little higher than you felt; also the left hand is higher than the right because it is tending to 'turn over' the right one. Notice that you did not perform that 'turn of the wrists' as it is called. You must not. It happens automatically. You will also see the left arm straight, and the right arm bent at the elbow, which is down. You did not consciously do that. You must not. It happens automatically.

Where is the club? The shaft is pointing rather backwards, and the face of the club is facing partway to the sky. You did not voluntarily put it into that position. Once more, you must not. It goes there automatically.

During a 'live' swing, the hands beyond this point, rise a little higher still, lifting the right elbow 'off the body'; and the impetus of the swing carries the club head farther back until it swings towards your back to point at the target, i.e. to your left.

The momentum of the swing in this final stage completes the gradual cocking of your wrists. You did not consciously do that. You must not.

Remember that all these things have happened, but you felt that you had merely swung your arms round to the right, flat, in a 'straight line' parallel to the floor, thus revolving your spine.

Now, swing in the same flat arc to the left and you will observe, to all intents and purposes, the same phenomena; that is, your hands have crossed and gone up, the right arm is straight while the left one is bent. You did not do these things voluntarily. Nor must you.

Actually there are slight differences when swinging to the left, all due to the fact that the left hand is higher on the club shaft.

Didn't you feel great power in that swing? But you did not feel very secure on your legs.

You have now executed the correct orthodox golf swing with the part of your body above the armpits; except that it should have been on an almost perpendicular plane, instead of, as it was, horizontal.

It will be noticed that in the upper part of the swing – i.e. of shoulders, arms, and club – there are many automatic occurrences; but in the lower part – i.e. of hips, legs, and feet – every movement is automatic.

It was the lower part of the swing which made you insecure on your feet, because it was entirely rotatory, which it should not be.

When the back is bent making the upper part of the spine almost horizontal, then the upper conscious part of the backswing is to the right and upwards; and the lower subconscious part of the swing moves in the same general direction before it is automatically forced into a part rotatory movement. This subtle difference produces a check to the end of the backswing and a consequent feeling of perfect balance.

The same rule applies to the forward swing, i.e. the upper conscious part is to the left and upwards, and the lower subconscious part moves in the same direction before turning to the left, thus ensuring good balance.

It can be accepted that if you set any part of your body in motion in a certain direction, the first movement of the remainder of your body will be in the same direction.

Prove this by swinging an arm around you, and observe your whole body twist in the same direction. Then swing an arm straight to one side and upwards, and your body will move in the same direction. You made only one purposeful movement; all the other movements were subconscious and compensatory; i.e. for the purpose of maintaining your balance. So it is with golf, the entire swing is performed by the upper part of your body – that part of your body to which your arms are attached. Grasp that fact.

THE CORRECT ATTITUDE

We will now briefly deal with the swing in the correct golfing attitude.

Stand upright, gripping a golf club which is parallel to the floor. For the next step don't move your shoulder joints so as to move your hands nearer to, or farther from, your body; and don't alter the shape of your wrists thereby altering the angle between your arms and the club shaft. Merely bend your back, particularly the upper part (see diagram No. 5), until the club head rests on the ground. You will then be in the correct and natural position for hitting a golf ball which is on the ground as described at the beginning of this chapter.

A good way of assuming this position and getting used to it, is to let the arms hang in front of the legs, and clear of them; then to look intently at a spot on the ground about two feet in front of you, as though you were a Scotsman looking for a penny, and consequently wanted to get your eyes nearer the ground! You will be surprised how big a golf ball looks when you look at it in this way.

Having struck the correct attitude, everything is plain-sailing. The backswing and the forward swing are performed in exactly the same manner as when you were standing erect, by revolving your shoulders around the upper part of your spine.

All the things that happened automatically when you stood erect, will occur automatically now; the only difference being that the swing will feel to be vertical and in a 'straight' line, instead of horizontal and rotatory; and that there is a check to the end of the backswing and the forward swing, in consequence of which you will feel secure on your feet.

THE FIRST FACTOR OF THE GOLF SECRET is that the upper part of the spine must be horizontal or nearly so, thus permitting a practically perpendicular revolving of the shoulders around it, to execute both the backswing and the forward swing; every movement in all parts of the body below this level, i.e. of hips, legs and feet, being entirely subconscious, compensatory and automatic.

CHAPTER 2

THE GOLF SECRET – SECOND FACTOR

THE LEFT SHOULDER

I CONSIDER the left shoulder to be the most important part of the anatomy used in the golf swing. If you think only of the left shoulder to the exclusion of everything else, you will play better golf than if you don't think of it, no matter what else you do.

I am convinced that the left shoulder alone consciously begins the backswing, and also begins the forward swing and contributes much of the force and power to it.

Before attempting to prove my contentions, it is necessary that the reader should have a very definite idea of what I mean by 'left shoulder', since it could mean any one of three things.

(1) I do not mean the shoulder joint, which is formed by the shoulder blade (the scapula) and the top end of the upper arm bone (the humerus). This joint is used when you wish to move the upper arm.

It is important to realize that without using the joint, its position in relation to the chest can be varied in three different ways.

(a) Upwards, as when you shrug your shoulders.
(b) Backwards, as when you brace your shoulders to produce a soldierly appearance.
(c) Forwards, as when you bring your shoulders forward and consequently nearer together, making yourself flat-chested. Incidentally, this is the position into which you should put your shoulders when addressing a golf ball.

(2) I do not mean the shoulder muscles which cover the shoulder joint, and bring it into action when you wish to move the upper arm.

(3) I mean the 'architectural' shoulder, which might be called the top left 'corner' of the body.

During the course of the golf swing, the shoulder joint position in relation to the chest is not altered, except involuntarily near the end of the backswing and again near the end of the forward swing: therefore for our purpose I would like the reader to regard it as being fixed to, and as being a part of, the chest.

A downward or upward movement of the shoulder (as defined) is a very complicated body movement, but there is no point in describing the many muscles involved because the movement is quite easily performed without the knowledge. The important thing is that the left shoulder is the 'point of concentration', and its movement can be easily visualised.

The Golf Swing Wheel

Now study diagram No. 6, which represents a golfer ready to begin the backswing, and is to be regarded as a wheel. For the sake of clarity the right arm is not depicted.

To start any wheel in motion the force is applied to the hub, then transmitted centrifugally through the spokes to the rim.

Since it is acknowledged by all that the spine (some say neck or head, which are extensions of the spine) is the hub of the golf swing, it is obvious that we must find the best method of making that hub revolve on its axis, to begin, and complete, the backswing and the forward swing.

To enable the club head to return to the ball on the forward swing, it is desirable to prevent the hub from changing its position (either upwards, downwards, forwards, backwards, or to right or left) in relation to the ball.

Backswing — First Movement

Since probably every authority with one exception agrees that the backswing is not begun with any part of the right side of the body, we can accept that.

For the moment I am leaving out of account such stunts as the 'forward press', which in any case should be regarded as an involuntary movement.

By reference to diagram No. 6 it will be seen that it is possible to set the hub revolving to the right, by moving any one of four portions of the total left arm; i.e. the hand, the forearm, the upper arm or the 'shoulder'. Let us consider what is likely to happen when beginning the backswing by these various agencies.

(1) The Hand. If you pick up any small article from a table you will see that your wrist will bend backwards as you do so. The same thing happens when you begin the backswing with your left hand, i.e. the wrist at once begins to 'break' or 'roll'. These are natural occurrences. So called 'hands first' is just the

opposite to this, and is an unnatural movement when concentrating on the hands, because it is in fact performed naturally by the left arm. This wrist-rolling or wrist breaking is condemned by all the experts. The reason why so many people do begin the backswing this way is because they consciously use the left hand. It must now be clear why the backswing should not be begun by either hand.

(2) **The Forearm.** Similarly, using the forearm would tend at once to bend the elbow. This is also natural and to be expected, but very undesirable so early in the backswing, as there can be no semblance of a straight left arm, and the swing would be anything but 'wide'.

(3) **The Upper Arm.** To begin the backswing with the left upper arm (which would be done by the shoulder muscles) would at once bring the left shoulder joint into action, before the left 'shoulder' had gone down. This could have several disastrous effects, viz.:

(a) Since the first movement would necessarily be in the shoulder joint, this would be making the shoulder, instead of the spine, the hub of the swing. The dangerous possibilities can be envisaged. Since the shoulder is bound to change its position on the backswing, this variable hub will produce a variable rim, or club head arc.

(b) Since the entire movement would be upwards from the start, the left 'shoulder' would be too high at the end of the backswing.

(c) The backswing of the arm and club head would be finished before the 'shoulder' had time to finish its backswing; i.e. you would not have the full shoulder pivot considered essential for a full shot by all experts.

The use of the left upper arm to begin the backswing is perhaps the commonest wrong method (which is also commonly thought to be correct), yet it has all the above-mentioned possible and undesirable consequences; and perhaps as many possible directions for the ball to travel, owing to incomplete shoulder turn and the left shoulder being too high. A frequent result would be to contact the ball from outside the line, thus producing a slice.

There is one fault common to all three above-mentioned methods of starting the backswing. None of them set the 'wheel' in motion by first causing the hub to revolve. Instead they first move the joint immediately above the part used; i.e. the hand moves the wrist, the forearm moves the elbow, and the upper arm moves the shoulder joint.

(4) The Shoulder. For our purpose the shoulder is a 'fixed point', firmly attached through the chest to the upper part of the spine, therefore any movement of the shoulder (*N.B.* not the joint) will at once cause the 'hub' to revolve. The left shoulder is the part to think of when we wish to begin the backswing. The advantages of this method will be more fully appreciated when we come to consider the sequence of events which accompanies it, but before doing that we must decide the exact direction in which we intend to move the left shoulder.

BACKSWING – DIRECTION OF LEFT SHOULDER MOVEMENT

We can begin this investigation by asking a question. What happens to the left shoulder during the course of the golf swing? The answer is: all sorts of things with the average golfer, but with first class players the left shoulder moves always in the same direction, and that is why they get a grooved swing with every shot.

Since we have shown that the upper part of the spine is horizontal, or nearly so, it must be obvious that to revolve it the first movement of the left shoulder must be downwards, perpendicularly or nearly so; and since on the backswing the left shoulder should finish in front of the neck 'pointing over the ball', it is apparent that it must travel through a quarter of a circle downwards and to the right. Naturally, when the left shoulder is in front of the neck, the right shoulder is behind. In other words the shoulders have been twisted around the upper part of the spine.

I assure you it is possible to go wrong on this apparently simple movement. If you think too much of the shoulder going to the right you are apt to turn it to the right too soon, i.e. before it has gone far enough down. This would restrict the shoulder turn, and leave the left shoulder too high at the end of the backswing.

In actual practice it will usually be found better to think only of 'left shoulder down', then, when it has gone down as far as it can, it is bound to turn to the right, if you keep the hub (the upper spine) in the same position. At the same time visualize that quarter circle.

The more nearly horizontal the upper spine is (say with a short club) then the more perpendicularly will the left shoulder go down. Geometrically, this should put the right shoulder perpendicularly above the left one, which, of course, it does not. Those who have learnt the previous chapter will know that this is because, after the upper part of the spine has 'tightened' to the right, then the lower more perpendicular part of the spine also tightens to the right; and in so doing it *turns* both shoulders, therefore the right one goes backwards and the left one forwards. It is lack of the knowledge of this twofold action of the spine that is responsible for so much confused thought and teaching. Because the left shoulder finishes in a forward position it is presumed that it has been consciously turned into that position. Do thoroughly understand this principle, because if the backswing starts right it is likely to finish right; and further, if the backswing is right the forward swing will probably be right.

It will now be apparent that the 'magic quarter circle' is on an inclined plane, downwards, forwards, and to the right; but remember that you merely push the left shoulder down, and that its apparent forward turn is due to the automatic hip turn. We can now formulate our second golden rule: *begin and complete the backswing by pushing the left shoulder down.*

Whether or not the reader is convinced that the backswing should be begun with the left shoulder, he will agree that it must traverse the path which I have outlined. When he admits that, he must also admit that the most certain way to make it do so is to push it down.

A full shoulder pivot is the most important need for any full shot, and failure in this respect the most common error. Left shoulder concentration will make a full shoulder pivot inevitable, so eliminating this common, fatal error.

BACKSWING – EXPERT CONFIRMATION

No matter what you may hear to the contrary, it is a fact that at the top of the backswing in the case of most of the world's leading players, the left shoulder is quite low down even when using the driver. Photographs in most pictorial golf books show the shoulder line to form an angle with the perpendicular, of approximately forty-five degrees.

It will be recalled that the left shoulder joint is subconsciously lifted to a higher level by the upswinging arm towards the end of the backswing. Prove this by feeling with your right hand, the outer end of your left collar bone rise, as you push your left arm upwards. But the left side of the chest does not rise. If you bear these two facts in mind when studying the above-mentioned shoulder line at the top of the backswing, you will realize that the 'top left hand corner of the body' is actually even farther down than it appears to be.

BACKSWING – EXPERTS' CONTRADICTORY BELIEFS

It is a fact that a dozen golf experts – including many all-time great players – have written books in which they each describe the commencement of the backswing differently. That is to say, no two descriptions are alike. Obviously at least eleven of them must be wrong! Only three of the twelve mention the left shoulder at all (they are on the right track), but since all their left shoulders must, and do, go down, it is just possible that they all begin the backswing with the left shoulder without being aware of it.

Some of these writers make the game even more complicated by describing different methods of starting the backswing with different clubs.

Don't take my word for the above statements. Compare the descriptions in the books you possess.

Don't make the game more difficult than it is: simplify it. Begin all shots with a downward movement of the left shoulder.

BACKSWING – EFFECTS OF CORRECT LEFT SHOULDER MOVEMENT

We must now study diagram No. 7, and consider the sequence of events which accrue from the downward movement of the left shoulder.

No. 9 (in diagram No. 7) represents the abruptly curved arc that results from incorrectly starting the backswing with hand or forearm.

The different positions of the component parts in figures 'A' and 'B' represent what happens during the early part of the backswing, when the shoulders correctly revolve around the horizontal upper part of the spine.

It should be clearly understood that whereas in an earlier section I described what a golfer should consciously do to start the backswing, I am now going to describe what subconsciously happens to the arms and the club in consequence.

As the left shoulder starts to go downwards the force is passed centrifugally through the 'spoke' to the 'rim' of the wheel, so that the club head is the last to move. As the left shoulder goes down, the right shoulder goes up the same distance. This carries the hands straight back to the right on the same level, therefore the club head also goes straight back on the same level (i.e. close to the ground as it should), consequently the arc is flattened and a wide swing is ensured. I do not mean to give the impression that that sequence of events will make a straight left arm a certainty, but there will be less tendency for the arm to bend, therefore there will be less difficulty in keeping it straight. That will tend further to widen the swing.

If you made the mistake of consciously pushing the club head back to the right close to the ground with your hand or arm, you would tend to sway, or even to look at the club head as it went back. Think only of your left shoulder, then the club head will automatically traverse its correct course.

When your left shoulder is half-way down, your hands and the club are about waist high. That is, the backswing is half completed without any conscious help from your arms. The part played by your arms, activated by the shoulder muscles, will be revealed in the next chapter.

A more complete description of the automatic occurrences will be given in the final chapter.

Forward Swing – First Movement

As was shown in the previous chapter, the forward swing is begun simply by revolving the shoulders around the horizontal upper part of the spine. The same rule applies (and for similar reasons) as in the backswing. That is, set the hub revolving by the nearest part of the left side of your anatomy to it, i.e. the left shoulder. A strong argument in favour of beginning the forward swing with the left shoulder is that as you performed the backswing with it, why transfer your concentration to another part of the body? In the split second necessary to execute the golf swing, you have not time to think of different things, either together or in sequence, therefore think only of the most vital – the left shoulder.

Forward Swing – Direction of Left Shoulder Movement

On the backswing the left shoulder traversed a quarter of a circle downwards and to the right. On the forward swing it retraces its steps on that quarter circle (hence the grooved swing) and continues the almost vertical circular motion until it is behind the neck, at which stage the right shoulder is under the chin. The head then turns left, and the whole body (both shoulders and head) moves to the left as the shot finishes.

The left shoulder then, travels at least a half circle. Get this 'magic half circle' well fixed in your mind and visualize it on every shot: left shoulder to the left, upwards, then to the right.

You have often heard of getting the left hip 'out of the way', but as we have demonstrated, it gets out of the way automatically. You have not heard of getting the left shoulder 'out of the way', which is very important for the following reason. Because the left hand is higher than the right one on the club shaft, in effect the left arm is three inches longer than the right arm. This additional length of left arm will 'block' the blow of the forward swing (resulting in a curtailed swing or follow through, or a bent left arm at impact) unless the left shoulder is 'got out of the way'. It is the half circle movement that gets the left shoulder out of the way. Get this point clear: as the hands and the club are going 'through the ball' followed by the right shoulder, the left shoulder is moving in the opposite direction, that is, to the right, away from the shot. It is probable that the last part of this half circle should be the fastest part, since it coincides with impact, or soon after, which is when the club head should be travelling fastest.

Just as you could go wrong on the backswing quarter circle, so you can go wrong on the forward swing half circle. If you should mistakenly concentrate on the movement to the left or right of the half circle, you will respectively carry too much weight to the left or keep it to the right. Whereas if you concentrate on the upward part of the half circle, provided you keep the hub in the same place and visualize the half circle, then the shoulder must move to the left first, and must move to the right after it goes up.

It amounts to this: since on the backswing the downward element in the movement of the left shoulder was the important part, so on the forward swing you must concentrate on its opposite, i.e. the upward part, to obtain a grooved swing.

This all seems so obvious that I almost blush to make such a fuss about it, but I know how vitally important it is, and yet I have never heard or read anything about it. You need only try what I have suggested to convince yourself of its truth.

It is important to realize that the inclined plane of the forward swing half circle (like that of the backswing quarter circle) is an illusion, and is due to the automatic turn of the hips, whereas the conscious plane of the shoulder movement is perpendicular, because the upper part of the spine is horizontal.

FORWARD SWING – SPEED OF SHOULDER MOVEMENT

After a momentary pause of the left shoulder in front of your neck at the top of the backswing, you should start, and complete, the forward swing as quickly as possible, by pulling your left shoulder up quickly. Don't think of beginning the forward swing slowly and gradually increasing the pace. You have no option but to begin slowly since you are reversing the direction, but since the forward swing is all over in a split second you must think of speed from the start. The more quickly you take your left shoulder up, the more quickly the club head will come down and through the ball, and the farther the ball will go. That quick shoulder movement is the 'quick turn of the shoulders' which has been described as occurring in all professionals. My repeated use of the word 'quick' is to impress its importance. Quick shoulder movement gives quick swing!

FORWARD SWING – LIKELY MISGIVINGS

(1) You may imagine that since, at the top of the backswing your left shoulder is pointing over the ball, to pull it upwards would push the club out to the right in an exaggerated inside-to-out swing. Actually it *is* this movement that produces the much vaunted inside-to-out swing – it ensures the club head staying 'inside the line' until near impact. But, there is another factor which prevents the inside-to-out swing being exaggerated.

Just as on the backswing all that you felt that you did was to swing on a straight line upwards to the right (the swing being carried around subconsciously by the automatic hip turn); so on the forward swing, all you feel that you do is to reverse the direction by swinging on a straight line upwards to the left – the automatic hip turn bringing your shoulders square to the ball at impact.

Every golf shot is a straight line shot!

(2) Don't let anyone tell you that swinging upwards will make you 'top' the ball. Diagram No. 7 shows how the coincident up and down movements of the right and left shoulders, together with the hands travelling onwards, flattens the arc of the swing at the bottom. This will prevent any rising of the club head before it should happen and therefore prevent topping.

(3) Thinking of performing the forward swing quickly from the start will not make you 'snatch', because you are not thinking of hands or club; they will take care of themselves, and in fact, will still be going 'backwards' as your left shoulder starts to go 'forwards'.

FORWARD SWING – EXPERT CONFIRMATION

Let us examine diagram No. 8 and note what is common to most experts. In it will be seen the approximate shoulder line of most professionals at, or soon after, impact. This is a composite diagram based on photographs in pictorial golf books of twenty-five expert golfers, mostly British and American professionals. There are, of course, variations of a few degrees either way with different players.

Figure 'A' (viewed from in front of the player) shows the angle formed by a line through the shoulders to be about forty-five degrees to the perpendicular.

Figure 'B' (viewed from the right of the player) shows the angle formed by a line through the shoulders to be only about twenty degrees to the perpendicular.

Both figures prove that the left shoulder is considerably higher at, and after, impact than at address; and also that it is definitely going upwards, and not turning to the left.

FORWARD SWING – EXPERTS' CONTRADICTORY BELIEFS

As we found with the backswing, twelve experts – including many all-time great players – have written describing the beginning of the forward swing, again, all differently. Therefore, at most, only one of them can be right! Two of these experts say, begin by transferring the weight, but neither explain how to do this. We have proved that pulling the left shoulder upwards causes automatic weight transference; and since we know that experts' left shoulders do go up, it seems likely that they all start the forward swing that way. As they have been unable to analyse the movement with any semblance of unanimity (compare their books), it is well that someone should do it for them!

Don't complicate the game: simplify it. Always begin the forward swing with an upward movement of the left shoulder.

FORWARD SWING – EFFECTS OF CORRECT LEFT SHOULDER MOVEMENT

Now that we know how to use the left shoulder to set the hub in motion, we can consider the automatic effects on other parts of the body, the club head and the ball.

Remember that when you begin the forward swing with the left shoulder, the arms and the club have not quite finished their backswing. These coincident movements, of the club 'backwards' and the left shoulder 'forwards', keep the upper part of the spine wound to the right. This fact (as the left shoulder starts to move) causes the left hip to move to the left and backwards (weight transference). This very obvious hip movement is the cause of the erroneous belief that the left hip begins the forward swing.

As the left hip goes backwards, the right hip, of course, comes forward, the combined movements constituting the unwinding and rewinding to the left of the lower more vertical part of the spine. This unwinding and rewinding process is passed upwards to the upper more horizontal part of the spine; thus allowing the left shoulder to accelerate its upward movement, which in turn hastens the descent of the arms towards the 'hitting area', with the wrists still cocked and the club shaft still bent. At the same time, the backward moving left hip has turned the shoulders to be square to the ball, and has also pushed the left heel on to the ground with a tendency for the foot to roll on to its outside edge. The left foot now becomes the fulcrum of the forward swing.

At this stage the effects of centrifugal force become apparent, and cause the 'rim of the wheel' to travel faster than the hub; consequently the hands and the club 'pass the body', wrist cocking (and 'elbow cocking' if present) having become automatically undone, so that the club head makes solid contact with the ball which moves off in a straight line at right angles to the left of the club face.

As the left shoulder continues its half circle, the hands and the club head go straight forward on the flattened arc, until they finally go upwards into a high finish, the delayed crossing of the right hand over the left taking place on the way. During this final phase, as the right shoulder passed under the chin, the head turned to the left, then the whole upper part of the body moved to the left to be supported by a firm left leg; the right leg having been dragged, so that the right foot rolled on to its inside edge before coming up more or less on its toe.

Note well: the only conscious action was to pull up the left shoulder. All the foot, leg and hip movements were automatic and secondary to the effort made with the upper part of the body, as was the downward movement of the arms. The wrist uncocking and subsequent hand crossing were also automatic and due to centrifugal force. The hands did nothing, except grip the club shaft.

Forward Swing – Convince Yourself

I will now ask the reader to prove for himself that pulling the left shoulder upwards does in fact cause the rest of the body to do what I have said.

Stand absolutely erect, then forcibly raise the left shoulder (by which I mean the 'left corner of the body' and not the shoulder joint). What happened without your assistance? The left hip moved straight to the left and upwards, making the left leg firm, and the weight transferred to the left. Lower the 'shoulder', and the hip and the weight will return to the original position.

Now bend your back until the upper part of your spine is about horizontal as we have learnt that it should be when playing golf. Again forcibly raise the left 'shoulder'. What happened then without your assistance? The weight transferred to the left, your left hip moved to the left, upwards and backwards 'out of the way', again making the left leg firm. Also the right hip and knee came forward a little and the right foot rolled on to its inside edge with a tendency for the heel to rise.

This is proof that when playing golf, the back should be bent, the forward swing should be started by pulling the left shoulder upwards, and that the entire hip, leg and foot portion of the swing is automatic, and secondary to the upward pull of the left shoulder.

Remember the twofold action of the spine! As in the backswing, it is want of this knowledge that accounts for all the confusion in explaining the beginning of the forward swing.

The reader may now convince himself that the forward swing should not only be commenced, but completed, mainly by concentrating on the left shoulder.

Stand erect, gripping a golf club, which will be parallel to the floor when held in front of you, as you did when acquiring the 'feel of the golf swing'. Now swing as you should when hitting a golf ball, fairly slowly to the right and as quickly as you can to the left, feeling all the time that the club shaft remains parallel to the floor.

First of all, try to detect which part of your body appears to start the swing to the left, i.e. the forward swing. I will be surprised if you don't agree that it is your left shoulder, or at least the left side of your body. If you are doubtful, repeat the swing, but definitely begin and finish the forward swing with your right arm. I think you will find that the blow is weaker, the swing less wide, with less follow through, and with a tendency for you to remain on your right leg.

Again repeat the swing, this time concentrating on the left shoulder. You will have a feeling of tremendous power, your weight will transfer well to the left, the swing will be wide, and the follow through complete.

Finally, repeat the swing in the same manner, but, having first bent your back until the club head rests on the ground in the way previously described. This time the swing will be upright, therefore your balance will be better, and you will more definitely recognize that you are leading the swing with your left shoulder, and not some other part of the left side of your body.

LIMBER-UP

Before leaving the subject of left shoulder action, a word on limbering-up will not be amiss. We have all seen players swinging reasonably well at daisies on the first tee, and then playing a dud shot. They would get better results if, instead of merely swinging the club, they would limber-up the shoulders while firmly gripping the club. Get that full, free movement of the left shoulder, alternately in front of, and behind the neck.

THE SECOND FACTOR OF THE GOLF SECRET, is that the left shoulder is the point of concentration in revolving the shoulders around the horizontal upper part of the spine in both the backswing and the forward swing, the movement being downwards on the backswing and upwards on the forward swing; all movement below the chest being secondary to this, and automatic.

CHAPTER 3

THE GOLF SECRET – THIRD FACTOR

Voluntary Use of Arms.
Choice of Method.
Direction of Arm Swing.
Expert Confirmation.
How to do it.
Short Shots.

IN the two preceding chapters I think I have proved that the body plays the major part in the golf swing, and provides most of its power.

All leg movements – in fact all movements below the chest – we are satisfied, are automatic.

It now remains to consider the action of the upper limbs in the golf swing, during which investigation several facts must be kept constantly in mind.

(1) Because the upper part of the spine, which is the hub of the swing, is practically horizontal, the swing feels as if it were in a straight line, i.e. straight up to the right then straight up to the left.

(2) The swing appears to go to some extent around the body, owing to the subconscious turning of the hips, which carries the shoulders around.

(3) On both the backswing and the forward swing the bottom of the arc is flattened by the simultaneous up and down movement of the right and left shoulders.

(4) The only conscious feeling, apart from the down and up left shoulder movements, is of swinging upwards on the backswing and upwards on the forward swing.

I have said, *ad nauseam*, that the upper part of the spine is the hub of the golf swing; but, inside that swing there are two other subsidiary hubs and swings. These two hubs are the two shoulder joints, and the two swings are of the arms (see diagram No. 9).

It will be realized that while the spine is the fixed hub, the shoulder joints are movable hubs; and therefore while the golf swing is in progress, the 'arm swings' and arcs together with their hubs, are being revolved in their entirety around the fixed main hub. One might say there are two swings within a swing!

It is, of course, possible to play good golf without any conscious use of the arms, in which case the body movement carries the arms part way up both on the backswing and the forward swing. Prove that now. You will find that the hands move from one side to the other through at least a half circle.

The second factor in the subconscious use of the arms is centrifugal force and momentum, which carries them a little higher.

The third factor is that with the intention to swing the club upwards by the body, the shoulder muscles which swing the arms through the shoulder joints will automatically come to your assistance, thus sending the hands still higher.

VOLUNTARY USE OF ARMS

Of course, it is possible to reinforce the swing by actively swinging the arms with the shoulder muscles, and thereby gain extra length. Long hitters undoubtedly do this. This active use of the shoulder muscles (which is often mistakenly thought to be use of the hands), introduces a stumbling-block to the acquisition of a well 'timed' swing. For good timing and a consequent good shot, the 'three swings' must be synchronized. That is to say, the arms must be swung at the correct time in relation to the main swing around the spine.

How can we best achieve this object? It will necessitate first of all deciding with which part of the total arm we are going to swing. It should be obvious that since we are going to swing the whole arm, we must first move the top end.

Just as, in the case of the spine, we set the main hub in motion by the nearest part to it, i.e. the left 'shoulder', so here, we must set this lesser hub – the shoulder joint – in motion by the nearest part to it, i.e. the upper arm, by means of the shoulder muscles.

However, for the benefit of the cynics and the die-hards who still think they swing with their hands, we will take a look at other possibilities. These people probably think that we eat, pick up a tumbler, box, fence, or play tennis or golf with our hands. They are just about as wide of the mark as possible. The hand is used merely to hold, or grip, the implement.

Go through any of these movements now, and see if you can detect your hand doing anything but 'holding on'.

Even a table is not thumped with the hand! The hand is merely the end of the arm which makes contact. You could pat it with your hand, which is what you do to a golf ball if you 'hit' it with your hands.

The chief muscles used for performing the above – especially when any effort is required as in playing golf – are those about the shoulders, which raise the upper arms. If anyone doubts that assertion, let him attempt to do any of those things while his upper arms are fixed to his chest by a rope, thus preventing his shoulder muscles from functioning.

It should be recalled that when we use any part of the arm, it causes a natural movement of the joint immediately above it, then if necessary for further effort, movement of the joint above that. For example, if you swing back a golf club with your left *hand* you will find that the wrist begins to 'bend' first, then the elbow, and finally the shoulder joint. These things tend to occur with either hand or with both together, whether on the backswing or the forward swing, with consequent narrowing of the swing. On the forward swing they cause too active wrist-work, with too early crossing of the right hand over the left, and a consequent likelihood of pulling the ball to the left. See diagram No. 10 which is, of course, diagrammatic, but serves to demonstrate these points. In practice the 'wrist and elbow swings' are a little wider than indicated owing to partial use of other joints.

I think everyone will now be convinced that the arms must be swung from the shoulder joints, by the shoulder muscles acting on the upper arms. By this means we will maintain the wide swing which we have initiated with the left shoulder.

CHOICE OF METHOD

Compare the two methods of using the arms, both on the backswing and the forward swing. If we allow the arms to function involuntarily and automatically, we will probably lose a little length! But the great problem of 'timing' will be solved, which is much more accurate if not interfered with by the voluntary use of the arms. That is to say, the main swing around the spine, and the two subsidiary swings 'around' the shoulder joints, become automatically synchronized. In consequence of this, there will be a greater number of accurately struck and therefore straight shots.

While accuracy is an advantage gained from involuntary arm movement, this has to be weighed against the advantages of conscious arm movement, which are fourfold.

(1) It probably makes you more aware of your arms, so forming a link between your left shoulder and the grip.

(2) It tends to stretch the arms, thus helping to keep the left one straight on the backswing, and downward beyond impact: and then the right one.

(3) It makes the hands go to a desirable higher level both on the backswing, and on the forward swing.

(4) Greater length probable.

The reader will later be better able to judge which method to adopt.

DIRECTION OF ARM SWING

If we decide to assist the swing by voluntarily using the arms, we must know in which direction to push or swing them, both on the backswing and the forward swing. It is obvious that this direction must be the same as that which the arms follow involuntarily, if left to themselves.

If the reader has learnt what has gone before he will know, without a doubt, that the direction is upwards on the backswing, then upwards on the forward swing, but I will give further proof.

It will be remembered that on the backswing the left shoulder goes down and to the right through a quarter circle, therefore obviously the hands must traverse a quarter circle to the right and upwards.

It will also be remembered that we had to concentrate on the downward element of the shoulder movement, therefore again obviously, we must concentrate on the upward part of the arm quarter circle. The downward movement of the left shoulder compels the left arm to move first to the right automatically, then the inevitable movement of the shoulder to the right allows the arm to go upwards.

The mere fact that the left arm and the club are going to the right side of the body, will automatically transfer all the weight that is necessary, whereas to concentrate on the movement of the arm to the right (as is implied by consciously taking the club head straight back behind the ball), would make you sway, and shift the main hub position, or transfer too much weight and probably have the hands too low at the top of the backswing.

If the reader will go through these movements with a golf club, he will notice that the left shoulder going down helps the arm and club to go up, and vice versa. That is because these two movements are really in the 'same' direction. They are on the same 'line', which will perhaps be better visualized as a groove.

I will again emphasize that all voluntary or conscious movement in the golf swing (or in any other muscular activity for that matter), must be in the same direction. See diagram No. 11, in which is shown the club head arc (the curve of which is partly due to subconscious wrist-roll), but mainly due to sub-conscious turn of the shoulders on the hips; also the actual hand arc (which will be less curved the more nearly horizontal the upper part of the spine); and also the feel of the hand arc, which, like the feel of the shoulder pivot, is in a straight line, or nearly so.

Some people correctly push the left shoulder down, then mistakenly swing the club around themselves to the right thus making the swing angular, and necessitating an alteration in the direction of the force. Surely this is obviously wrong!

Therefore if you admit that the left shoulder should go down, you must also admit that the left arm and the club should go up.

Regarding the direction of the forward swing, this must be the reverse of the backswing. 'Downswing' is a misnomer which suggests finishing the shot at impact, and in fact, causes many players to do so, and also to 'dip' the body and hit the ground behind the ball.

As the left shoulder goes up, the hands and the club must come down, hence the *down* stroke although you are swinging up. With irons the ball is contacted before the ground merely because it is behind the lowest point of the arc.

We have already satisfied ourselves that the left shoulder going upwards leads the forward swing into the 'groove' which it traversed on the backswing, and also causes the arms and the club to automatically come down into the 'hitting area'.

It is from here that the active part of the forward swing actually begins – although you should think of it as beginning at the top – therefore the 'hit' should follow the left shoulder, upwards. Only thus can you keep the swing, as it should be, in a 'straight' line.

There must be no pulling around the left side of the body, which may occur as a result of trying to swing parallel to the ground (i.e. keeping the club head close to the ground), and which would keep the left shoulder too low at impact.

The feeling should be of trying to send the ball well above the target. In fact the higher you try to send the ball the farther it will go. It will also go higher, but only towards the end of its trajectory since it is travelling uphill all the way, at right angles to the face of the club.

Most experts say that the club head is travelling its fastest after impact. Surely the direction of the fastest movement – which soon after impact must be upwards – must also be the direction of the forward swing. I know the fantastic view has been expressed that the club head floats onwards faster after we have stopped hitting, but I cannot think that any intelligent man can accept that.

We must be hitting when the club head is travelling fastest, i.e. after impact.

Diagram No. 12 shows the position of fastest speed of club head and also of arms and hands. The arms moving onwards help to flatten the bottom of the arc even though the feel of the swing is upwards. The speed of the onward moving hands together with the hitting upwards, also keeps the face of the club square to the target during this period, thus delaying the automatic crossing of right hand over left until well after the ball has gone.

Finally, the left shoulder going upwards and the hitting upwards in the same direction, plus the fact that the left hand is higher than the right one on the club shaft, produces automatically the inside-to-out forward swing, which is almost universally considered desirable.

Expert Confirmation

(1) There are in existence many photographs of experts at the top of the backswing, in which the left foot is merely rolled on to its inside edge, without any heel raising at all. Try a backswing now, and see if you can get your left foot into that position by swinging your left arm in any other direction than upwards. I know you cannot.

You will find swinging the arm upwards a perfectly natural movement if you first make the upper part of your spine about horizontal. You will also find that the less horizontal that part of your spine, the more inclination there will be for your left heel to rise. Any left heel raising that does occur should be subconscious, and due to the automatic turn of the hips, and should occur towards the end of the backswing. Finally, if you make the mistake of swinging around yourself, your left heel will rise much too much, and you will consequently feel unbalanced.

(2) There are some, but fewer, photographs showing the same position on the right foot after impact. Fewer because the rolling action of the foot due to hitting upwards is soon masked by the heel raising which has to occur owing to the much greater momentum of the forward swing.

(3) There exist a few photographs of experts at impact with both heels off the ground. If the reader will swing a club and definitely hit down, he will find that he cannot possibly get into that position. In my opinion the players I have quoted are hitting correctly upwards, but they have made the mistake of using the arms before the body, which caused the right heel to rise before the body had pushed the left hip back, and the left heel down.

(4) At, or soon after, impact, in the case of most professionals the left shoulder is much higher than at address. That means that the left shoulder is going upwards and not turning left, therefore the direction of the forward swing must be the same, that is, upwards. In my opinion, some of the extreme examples of this nearly perpendicular line of the shoulders to be seen in photographs, could not be maintained so far into the 'follow through' unless the forward swing were directly upwards, as though an attempt was being made to hit the ball into the sky well above the target.

(5) There are lots of photographs of experts, with the club head as much as twelve inches past impact position, which show (in addition to the above-mentioned shoulder line), a total absence of wrist-roll, and the club face square to the target exactly as at impact. I maintain that this position of the hands

and the club face one foot past impact, is impossible to attain unless the player is hitting upwards. Don't take my word for it, try now to get the club face into that position without hitting upwards.

You will probably be told that that may occur, but only with the 'new' American swing. But the American swing is not new. Some of the photographs that I have in mind are of British experts, and at least one was probably taken twenty years ago.

A modification of this 'impact position' after impact, is when the player's wrists 'hinge' instead of remaining firm, which is even more proof of hitting upwards. There are several examples of this to be seen in golf books.

(6) It is always said, 'Let the club head follow the ball'. Does the ball not go upwards? How better can we 'let' the club head follow the ball than to make it do so by hitting upwards?

(7) Many professionals say, let the driver contact the ball as the club head is rising. If you hit as the club head is rising you must be hitting upwards.

(8) Some professionals admit to feeling no difference in the swings with woods and irons, with which I entirely agree. This puts all clubs in the same category as the driver in No. 7, above, so far as swinging upwards is concerned. Of course with irons the ball is contacted as the club head comes down, but merely because it is behind the bottom of the arc. The swing is not thereby affected.

(9) Many professionals advocate the hands being high, both at the top of the backswing and after the forward swing – when the shot is finished. Surely for the hands to go high they must go upwards, and what better method of ensuring their being high than to hit upwards?

How to Do It

Having established the fact, I think beyond doubt, that both the backswing and the forward swing must be upwards, it now remains to show how to do it.

Grip a golf club with the left hand only, and without deliberately lowering the left shoulder, do a backswing from the shoulder joint, i.e. swing straight up with the upper arm. Stop at the top, and examine yourself. You will find that the left shoulder is too high, the shoulder pivot is incomplete, and the club shaft is above your neck and pointing to the left of the target.

Now repeat that backswing, by a downward motion of the left shoulder, followed immediately by swinging the left arm from the shoulder joint, straight up. Stop at the top and again examine yourself. You will find the left shoulder low down, and pointing over the 'ball', with a full shoulder pivot, and the club shaft above your right shoulder, i.e. farther 'back' than before, and pointing to the target. All these details are just as they should be.

Now repeat the backswing while gripping the club with both hands, but apart from gripping the club don't let the right arm do anything. That is, do the backswing entirely with the left shoulder and arm as before, and the right arm in all its parts will automatically assume its natural and correct position.

It will be remembered that on the backswing the arms are automatically carried nearly half-way up, before the left arm starts its swing. How do I reconcile this with my advice to begin the arm swing immediately after the left shoulder begins to go down. The explanation is simple. It requires time for a thought to be transformed into action, therefore if you delayed thinking of the arm swing until when it should begin, you would be too late putting it into operation.

Conversely, by starting, i.e. thinking of starting, the arm swing immediately the left shoulder has put the main swing into the groove, you will commence the action rhythmically at the right time and place.

Apropos of this delayed action, it is now a proven fact. Continuous research into delay and reaction times proves that when a motorist decides to apply the brake, one-third to half a second elapses before he does so, even in a dire emergency.

Comparably, since it cannot take more than one second to perform the backswing, if you decide actively to swing up the left arm immediately after the left shoulder has started the backswing, you will not actually do so until the swing is about half completed.

As a matter of fact, after reasonable practice, when 'left shoulder down' has become habitual, it may be feasible to think of both movements – left shoulder down and left arm up – as beginning together, since the two movements – being in the same direction – are inseparable.

All that has been said about the backswing – including the comparison with the autotest car-driver – applies equally to the forward swing. Therefore begin the forward swing by pulling the left shoulder upwards as quickly as possible until it has completed at least a half circle and is behind the neck.

Concurrently with this movement, the left shoulder muscles acting on the left upper arm, will automatically assist the swing, since you have the intention to hit, and especially since your thoughts are concentrated on your left 'shoulder' dominating the swing.

Immediately the left shoulder begins to go upwards into the 'groove', you should consciously and with intent hit upwards with your right upper arm. Owing to the delayed action of maybe half a second, you will not actually hit until about half-way down, i.e. in the hitting area, before which of course you could not hit upwards.

The importance of thinking of hitting, and of thinking of speed, from the start of the forward swing will now be apparent. As on the backswing, it might prove desirable, with practice, to think of both movements – left shoulder up and hit upwards with right upper-arm – simultaneously.

SHORT SHOTS

All that I have said, in this and the two preceding chapters, refers in particular to any full shot, with whatever club it is played, from a driver down through the spoon, to iron shots including most shots from the rough, and even to a niblick explosion shot from a bunker. In all, by so doing, the club head will go 'through' the ball.

Regarding part shots, i.e. anything less than a full shot, maybe some elaboration is desirable.

I believe that every shot, from a drive to a putt, should be played, in effect, the same way. That is, the backswing should always be begun with a downward movement of the left shoulder, and the forward swing always with an upward movement of the left shoulder. Further, that every shot should be hit upwards by the right arm immediately after the forward swing has commenced. By this means, the weight will always transfer as it should – much or little – automatically.

Think of all part shots as 'fractions' of a drive, and if you wish to play a three-quarter, half, or quarter shot, do not try to do so by limiting the distance which your hands or the club head travel. That is too vague and will only result in hesitation and uncertainty, particularly as it necessitates transferring your attention from your left shoulder to your hands and the club, and back again to the left shoulder, all in a split second. It cannot be done – successfully! Instead, always think of the left shoulder.

For a quarter shot let the shoulder go down a quarter of the way: for a half shot, half-way; and for a three-quarter shot, three-quarters of the way.

These distances cannot of course be gauged accurately, but they serve to demonstrate the principle of restricting all movements equally. That is to say, the shorter the shot the less shoulder pivot and the less body movement generally. That is what professionals mean when they erroneously say 'no body movement with chip-shots'. Actually the body movement should always be felt even if it is imperceptible to the onlookers; and don't forget that the only conscious, active, movement is of the left shoulder (and maybe of the left upper arm on the backswing, and the right upper arm on the forward swing), all other movements – of hips, legs, feet, and including the desired limitation of the backswing – will occur subconsciously.

Remember also, that with most of these part shots, the forward swing should be practically the same as for a full shot, because you are still hitting upwards after impact just as with a full shot. Therefore begin the forward swing by pulling the left shoulder up and let it uninterruptedly complete its half circle to behind the neck.

The exception to this rule would be the very short shot, say a chip or short pitch, which might be played slowly. There would then be no need for a full 'follow through', but even so, it would be wise to visualize that full finish, thus to ensure the left shoulder and consequently the club head traversing the correct arc.

As with full shots, the right arm should 'come in' at the right time, i.e. after the left shoulder has determined the groove.

Many players prefer to play very short shots 'all right-handed.' While it is true that the shorter the shot the less harm there will be from doing this, because the hands are not above the 'hitting area' where the right arm *should* come in, nevertheless many shots are fluffed by concentrating on the right side of the body because this tends to delay or prevent weight transference to the left.

With all these short shots, including putts, much better results will be obtained by concentrating on the left shoulder to begin the forward swing, then all the body will be moving, as it should be, however slightly, in the same direction.

To some people, concentration on the left shoulder will no doubt seem too remote from the club head for very short shots. For them, the rule to hit upwards with the right arm (or hand if they prefer to think of it that way), must be doubly remembered, because the left shoulder will not then be leading the swing into the correct groove. Instead, the right arm – if the blow is upwards – will tend to push the left shoulder into the groove; also there will be only little danger because the left shoulder will have come down only slightly.

Incidentally, it is this almost imperceptible movement of the left shoulder, and consequently of the body also, that is the cause of some professionals believing that there is no body movement in putting. They are wrong.

THE THIRD FACTOR OF THE GOLF SECRET is the sensation of swinging directly upwards, both on the backswing and the forward swing; the left 'shoulder' being assisted by the left and right shoulder muscles swinging the upper arms, either subconsciously or consciously.

CHAPTER 4

GOLF FALLACIES – IN TRUE LIGHT

Use and Misuse of –
Words.
The Mind.
The Body.
The Head.
The Legs and Feet.
The Arms.
The Hands.
The Fairway.

IN describing the three factors of the golf secret, I have intentionally omitted many details of what happens during the course of the swing – such as wrist-cocking, stopping at the top, and timing – so as not to confuse the issue.

Among the missing links now to be considered, some have already been touched upon where appropriate, while most have hitherto been considered to be controversial matters – even by the experts – and consequently have contributed to the prevalent contradictory teaching.

If you swing as I have described, most of the 'do's' and 'don'ts' of golf can be forgotten. The 'do's' will occur automatically. The 'don'ts' will not happen.

USE AND MISUSE OF WORDS

This involves criticism of the expressions 'backswing', 'downswing', 'hitting down', and 'follow through'.

According to my beliefs, none of these give the correct impression of what a golfer is trying to do.

A golf club swung backwards and forwards by a person in the correct golfing attitude, describes approximately a circle, going up to the right and up to the left, with the greatest force, in both cases, past the bottom of the arc. That is, it is the same on both sides of the address position so why use different names which suggest that the force is applied in different positions and directions?

The simplest, most apt, and most descriptive terms are 'right upswing' and 'left upswing'.

These expressions describe exactly what the player should feel he wishes and intends to do.

'Backswing' suggests – and causes – either swinging around the entire body too rotatory and too flat; or, too far straight back on the reverse target line, tending to cause swaying, too much weight transference, and too upright a swing.

'Downswing' suggests – and causes – hitting downwards and staying down, and probably lurching because the left shoulder has not been 'got out of the way'. Also the shot tends to finish soon after impact similar to a tennis 'chop-shot'. Other possible results are, staying on the right leg, and hitting the ground behind the ball, or coming from outside the line, thus pulling the ball to the left, or slicing it.

'Hitting Down' with iron clubs produces the same wrong impressions and faults as 'downswing'.

With iron clubs the ball *is* hit as the club head comes down, but simply because it is behind the bottom of the arc. The forward swing is not thereby altered, but is still upwards.

Many professional writers now use the term 'Forward swing' instead of 'Downswing'. They, at least, are moving in the right direction but they haven't gone far enough. I would go farther and say 'left upswing'.

'Follow Through' ceases to have any meaning if you think of 'left upswing', since it then becomes what it really is, only an inevitable part of the correct forward swing.

Whilst registering my disapproval of the terms in common usage because they are harmful, I have used the terms 'backswing' and 'forward swing', so as to avoid confusion in reading. 'Downswing' and 'hitting down' I will not use.

USE AND MISUSE OF THE MIND

This involves a consideration of 'relaxation', 'concentration', and 'tension'.

In most golf books, in my opinion, there is a lot of misinformed talk about these subjects. Briefly, they all say 'relax and concentrate but have no tension'.

As I understand the meaning of these words, nobody can relax and concentrate at the same time; nor can anyone concentrate without tension, in fact these two are almost synonymous.

'Relaxation' implies a lessening of voluntary bodily and mental function, i.e. soft muscles and a blank mind.

'Concentration' calls for the opposite qualities, i.e. a sense of alertness of body and mind, in consequence of which, the person is, of necessity, in a state of 'tension'.

To say 'relax and concentrate' is comparable to commanding a horse to 'whoa, gee-up'.

It is a fact that before any muscular effort, the muscles to be used become taut, i.e. acquire 'tension'. For example, there is a long slender muscle in the calf of the leg, which commonly snaps in tennis players, if, caught unawares (i.e. relaxed), they make a sudden effort to retrieve the ball. That is why a tennis player should be always alert, on the *qui vive*, tense, concentrating – anything but relaxed – and literally, 'on his toes'.

Another example of concentration or tension is the indignant hero in a novel who 'clenches his fists and teeth', and 'sets his jaw'. I am sure that actors are taught to do these things when portraying anger.

This 'anger' is closely allied to the concentration needed in golf. Aren't you, in a way annoyed with the golf ball in wishing to hit it hard? And have you ever felt relaxed when annoyed or angry? No, annoyance, anger, or concentration has the opposite effect – it produces tension, a tautening of muscles and a desirable firmer grip. At least one professional has written – in effect – that annoyance can improve golf. That has also been my experience, and I believe it is due to the consequent increased 'tension – concentration' and accompanying firmer grip.

As a final example, most people must have noticed when reading an exciting book, or watching a thrilling film, how through concentration their whole body becomes tense, their muscles contracted, their heart beating stronger and faster, even to the extent of causing headache, and later preventing sleep.

It is beyond my comprehension how anybody can believe that a 'relaxed' body can propel a golf ball three hundred yards. Also, the facial contortions of many professionals when wielding a golf club, suggest to me a very high degree of tension.

Concentrate at golf you must – as with any other purposeful activity. A very firm grip is the key to concentration.

USE AND MISUSE OF THE BODY

This calls for comment on 'the shape of the body at address', 'the backswing', 'the forward swing', 'the inside-to-out forward swing', 'pressing', 'the stop at the top', 'timing', and 'golf exercises'.

Shape of the Body. Professional writers often say 'stand erect', 'don't stoop', or, 'there must be no overhanging of the upper part of the body'. But diagram No. 4 plainly shows that most experts have the upper part of their spines about horizontal at address.

Shape of the Swing. Whether the swing is flat or upright should depend entirely on the degree of back-bending. The more nearly horizontal the upper part of the spine, the more upright the swing. That is why the swing with short clubs is more upright than with long ones.

Also that is why the swing should always feel the same. There should be no deliberate attempt to swing more upright or more flat. Merely swing correctly by revolving the shoulders.

Backswing. The backswing should be begun by the left shoulder moving the body (assisted actively or subconsciously by the left arm through the shoulder muscles), thus setting the hub (upper spine) in motion.

Forward Swing. The forward swing should be begun by the left shoulder moving the body, assisted subconsciously by both arms – maybe consciously by the right one – through the shoulder muscles. The forward swing like the backswing, is essentially a revolving of the shoulders around the horizontal upper part of the spine.

Inside-to-out Forward Swing. Providing the body and the swing are the correct shape as already described, and the swing is correctly executed, then the forward swing will be – inevitably – from inside-to-out, without the player trying to make it so.

If both hands were at the same level on the club shaft, then the backswing and the forward swing would be identical and 'parallel' to the target line. But, because the left hand is higher so is the left shoulder, which produces a slight curving of the left side of the body. This anatomical adjustment compels the backswing to come somewhat inside the line, then if the forward swing is performed correctly by pulling the left shoulder upwards and hitting upwards, it is bound to be inside-to-out.

Therefore to make a conscious effort to swing from inside-to-out is to court disaster since you will then swing too much inside-to-out.

Pressing. Professionals and their books almost invariably say 'don't press', which can only mean 'don't hit hard'. This mistaken advice comes from a wrong conception of the direction of the hit. Hitting downwards, or even 'forwards', when 'pressing' or hitting hard, causes lurching and movement of the head to the left. But if the swing is visualized as a circle, and moving fastest after impact, which will necessitate hitting upwards, then you can – and should – press, i.e. hit as hard as you can.

By pulling the left shoulder up and then to the right, through its half circle – thus getting the left shoulder 'out of the way' – all the pressing you can produce can do no harm.

Many years ago I asked one well-known player to tell me the 'secret'. He replied, 'Just hit the ball hard.' He won a very major tournament the same year!

I am sure there has been too much gentle golf taught, and the wrong impression given by such mistaken expressions as 'grip lightly', 'no tension', and 'swing slowly and let the club head do the work'. I believe that teaching belongs to the day when tennis was 'lawn tennis'; and table tennis was 'ping-pong'. Both these games are now aggressive, as I believe golf should be.

It is time for a little of 'grip the club as tightly as you feel you should to knock the ball out of sight'. I recommend this hard hitting even for the beginner.

Stop at the Top. Should there be a conscious stop at the top of the backswing? Yes, definitely! All are bound to agree that it is impossible to reverse a car or to make anything else change its direction without first stopping, if only momentarily. The same rule applies to a golf club.

But the golf swing, as distinct from the golf club, needs a little more consideration. I am quite sure that at no time during the full golf swing does the entire body and the golf club become stationary, but all the different parts of this ensemble do stop in a very definite order.

The backswing having begun, the left shoulder is the first part to stop, when it should be in front of the neck; then the whole of the left arm, from shoulder to wrist, stops; then the hand stops on completion of wrist-cocking; and finally the club head stops when the impetus of the swing has 'bent' the club shaft.

While, say, momentum is still causing the hand to cock the wrist, the left shoulder is beginning the forward swing by going upwards into its half circle groove, and the left hip is moving to the left and backwards; by which time the hands have automatically come down into – or towards – the hitting area, with the wrists by now fully cocked or just starting to automatically uncock; the club shaft being by now fully bent.

That is to say, the order in which these four parts stop prior to reversing, at the end of their individual backswings, is the same as the order in which they started it – left shoulder, arm, hand, club head.

There are three very obvious reasons for this order.

(1) One would expect the finish to be in the same order as the beginning, because the earlier starters have a 'start' on the others.

(2) The relative distances the four parts have to travel on the backswing would make it likely that the shorter journey of the shoulder would end first.

(3) By no other order of stopping at the top could you get rhythm into the swing. Obviously, the first part to stop must be the first part to start again in the reverse direction. Also, these 'four points of pressure' in developing the speed of the forward swing, must be applied in sequence, beginning with the leading part, i.e. the left shoulder.

Visualizing these occurrences, it is plain to see how the speed of the forward swing is gradually – though automatically – built up and increased; and that the player must not interfere with the rhythm by attempting to increase the speed at any given point, as is so often erroneously advocated.

Also it is plain to see why chaos results from 'pulling on the rope from the middle' by starting the forward swing with arm or hand.

Until it becomes second nature to do a full shoulder pivot by forcing the left shoulder downwards through its quarter circle, there is a way by which you can be sure of completing the movement, and also of ensuring the correct 'stop at the top'.

When commencing the backswing, while looking at the ball, the left shoulder gradually comes into the field of vision. That is to say, if you think about it you can see the shoulder without taking your eyes off the ball, and you can actually see when it stops, before which you should not begin the forward swing.

You would probably not attempt this feat when actually playing, but I can assure you it is well worth while when practising.

When playing 'part shots' or short shots – whether with short clubs or with the hands 'down the stick' – there is a very important point regarding the length of time to 'stop at the top'. I think it will be agreed that the longer the backswing the greater the momentum! Therefore in a short shot there will be less momentum and consequently a longer time will be required for the automatic wrist-cocking which the momentum produces. Consideration, and understanding, of these facts leads us naturally to the formation of a rule which will greatly improve anybody's 'short game', viz.: 'THE SHORTER THE SHOT THE LONGER THE STOP'.

It is impossible to give details of how long to stop, but on very short shots, including putts, I believe it is best to determine not to begin the forward swing until the entire backswing – including that of the 'wrists' and the club head – is complete, and therefore all backward movement stopped.

In my opinion, this 'waiting for the wrists to cock' is a much better and safer method than deliberately cocking the wrists, as advocated by many professionals. Conscious wrist-cocking is wrong, as it introduces a different movement into the swing, since it must be done with the hands – therefore it makes the game needlessly more difficult – and produces too much wrist-cocking. It is a mistake to aim at a lot of wrist-cocking for a short shot. Every movement will be automatically reduced in proportion to the length of backswing.

Finally, when playing any shot – even a full one – if a player experiences difficulty in starting the forward swing with the left shoulder before the other parts of the backswing are completed, he will be well advised to make a deliberate – though momentary – stop, at the end of the entire backswing, rather than feel that there is no stop, so long as he does begin the forward swing with the left shoulder. Indeed, if you are past the 'first blush of youth' you will probably get better results by this method of regarding the backswing and the forward swing as two separate entities.

Timing. A beloved word of the professionals is 'timing', but they usually wrap it in mystery. I have not seen it correctly defined, much less explained. As I see it, 'timing' is best described as 'rhythm', easy to understand, and easily acquired.

We will consider it under three headings.

(1) There must be synchronization of the two arm swings with the body swing through the three hubs, i.e. the two shoulder joints and the upper part of the spine. This will include the undoing of all 'joint-cocking' at impact. Visualize the uncocking (or unwinding) of the wrists, also of the left elbow joint if bent, and the left shoulder carrying the left arm down on the forward swing.

I will anticipate the readers' question, how is this to be achieved? It will all happen automatically if you obey my second injunction below, and allow the upper arms to 'come into' the shot subconsciously, although with practice you might assist voluntarily with the right upper arm.

(2) Get rhythm into the swing by beginning it with the leading part, i.e. the left shoulder.

(3) The time relationship between the backswing and the forward swing is most important in producing rhythm, so we will consider this in some detail. Players are usually told to swing back slowly, but it has often been observed that most experts do not swing back slowly. True enough, many don't, but if they swing back quickly, they swing forward more quickly; and that is why they drive the ball prodigious distances. There must be that difference in speed on the backswing and the forward swing.

Now we can see that this correct time relationship between the back and forward swings, in conjunction with concentration on the left shoulder, produces rhythm, which in turn produces, synchronization of the 'three swings', and therefore good timing.

The best example of good timing to watch, is a child

(preferably over five years of age) throwing a stone into the sea. He doesn't think of when his wrist cocks or uncocks! Watch how the body turns first, and how much more quickly the arm comes forward than it went back.

In parenthesis, the average woman throws a stone only a few yards from her right shoulder joint – and misses the target! Any man can throw a stone – we all learnt as boys. Women golfers please note! Try it now, and note the different speeds of the back and forward swings. Note also the definite 'stop at the top' before the throw, i.e. the forward swing. Also notice that your body begins to move, and weight to transfer, without consciously using your legs, before the arm comes forward; and lastly, that you don't give your wrist a thought.

If, when playing golf, you find that you are mis-timing your shots, you can easily recall this rhythm, even without your opponent knowing what you are doing.

As you walk round the course, swing a club with your right hand only, as though you were throwing a stone – but 'throw it away' upwards. You will then soon be timing your shots correctly.

Golf Exercises. The most important exercise to a golfer who values his health, is one that counteracts the deformities which golf tends to cause.

The left shoulder being permanently higher than the right one usually signifies a lateral curvature of the spine, called 'scoliosis'.

'Round shoulders' indicate an increase in the normal forward curve of that part of the spine, called 'kyphosis'.

As kyphosis increases it tends to obliterate the normal forward 'lumbar curve' of the spine at waist level.

Any such spinal deformity renders the development of osteo-arthritis of the spine (which is painful and incapacitating) more likely in later life. The deformity causes the arthritis by improper or imperfect alignment of adjacent joint surfaces.

The exercises to be described are simple, and consist of bending your body in the opposite direction to which golf tends to bend it.

To counteract the high left shoulder of the address and impact positions, stand erect, put your right arm straight above your head, and push the left arm down by the side of the left leg as far as you can, so that the two arms form practically one perpendicular line. Do the right side too, but concentrate on the left side.

To counteract the round shoulders which tend to develop in regular players who correctly bend their backs, bend your whole body backwards into the opposite position to the 'crouching attitude' of golf.

First twist your arms 'outwards', then push your shoulders backwards, then bend your neck by pushing your head as far back as you can, then bend the upper part of your spine backwards so that your chest comes up and forwards, then go as far back as you can, thus increasing the normal lumbar curve. Incidentally this exercise will increase your chest measurement and reduce your waist measurement, but will not, of course, improve your golf except in so far as you may feel better from having a better 'carriage'.

As a matter of fact you will probably play better golf by allowing the deformities to develop, because you will then more easily 'drop into' the address position; but it will be a different story when the arthritis ensues.

The most important, and probably, the most difficult movement in golf, is to get a full shoulder pivot with only little movement of the head.

It follows, therefore, that the most important exercise to improve golf is to twist the upper part of the spine, including the part in the neck.

Turn your head to look alternately over your left and right shoulders. At first, do it slowly, forcing your head as far round as you can, and try gradually to increase the range. Later, do it quickly as it should happen in the golf swing. Then, do it the other way round, i.e. keep your head still and turn your shoulders as you did your head.

Now, do the same thing while standing in the golfing attitude, always thinking of left shoulder down, and up. At first do it slowly, forcing alternately the left and right shoulders 'under the chin'; then do it in the proper golf swing tempo.

At this stage incorporate the arms by pushing the left upper arm up from the shoulder joint as the left shoulder goes down, then the right upper arm up from the shoulder joint as the left shoulder goes up.

Lastly, repeat the exercise while gripping a golf club, but do grip it tightly.

Incidentally I would ask you to notice how the wrists function when you don't think about them, but think only of your left shoulder.

You will notice that the variations of this simple exercise are constructive, in that they improve your swing at the same time as they exercise. They also, incidentally, give your arms and legs all the exercise they need.

The second important golf exercise is of the muscles of your hands and especially those of the forearms with which you grip the club. For that, you need only grip the club shaft while doing the other exercise – but do grip it with all the strength you possess.

It boils down to this – the best exercise for golf, is golf, but it must be correct golf, so as to train and develop the correct muscles and also the correct feel of the swing.

USE AND MISUSE OF THE HEAD

This involves discussion of 'eye on the ball', 'head turning', 'head still', 'head down', 'head up', 'topping', and 'slicing'.

These attributes and faults are inseparable in discussion so will be considered together to avoid repetition.

Actually, if you make the upper part of your spine horizontal and swing by revolving your shoulders around it as already instructed, then the attributes will be yours, and the faults will not happen.

'Head still', 'head down', 'head up', 'topping' and 'slicing', can all be disposed of very briefly for the following reasons. ·

(1) The head cannot be held 'still' because it must turn, first to the right then to the left, otherwise you will restrict the backswing and the forward swing (*vide ante*).

(2) 'Holding down' the head to prevent 'head up', will also prevent it from turning, as it must not be *held* down. Swing as instructed and it will *stay* down.

(3) 'Head up' is chiefly due to standing too erect. With proper back bending a player is much more likely to turn his head on its own axis than to be guilty of 'head up'. Even if this turning is done too early, in the player's anxiety to see where the ball is going, it will not raise the head or the arc of the swing; therefore he is much less likely to 'top' or 'slice' the ball.

When 'head up' occurs, the upper part of the body, including the hands and therefore also the club head arc, also come up, consequently the ball is topped, or missed. Alternatively, if the head goes up earlier in the forward swing, the left shoulder will turn to the left throwing the club head across the 'line', which, coming to the ball from outside-to-in will produce a slice.

So bend your back and you will practically have beaten the two commonest and most disastrous faults in golf.

Regarding 'head turning', as previously stated, to get the very important full shoulder pivot on the backswing, you must either let your left shoulder push your head round on its axis, or turn it to the right before beginning the backswing.

In the 'pushing method', when the upper part of the spine including that in the neck, is fully twisted, it must be obvious that if the head is not allowed to turn, a full shoulder pivot is impossible.

On the forward swing the same thing applies; when the right shoulder is approaching the chin, the upper spine being tightly twisted, the head must turn to the left. Again it must be obvious that if you do hold your head back ('head down', 'head still', or 'eye on the ball' too long), it is bound to act as a brake on the forward swing by restricting the shoulder turn.

If you 'turn the head' to the right (pointing the chin as it is called) before you start the backswing, you really put your head into the position where your left shoulder would have pushed it. Therefore by this method you can get a full shoulder pivot without further movement of the head to the right. That is the reason for this manoeuvre, and not any of the other peculiar suggestions that have been made. I have even read that it is done to enable you to look at the ball with your left eye! You should see the ball with both eyes.

To make sure that you are seeing the ball with both eyes, address the ball, turn your head to the right, then shut your left eye. If you cannot then see the ball, it means that your nose is in the line of vision of your right eye, and that you have turned your head too far to the right. Therefore turn it back until you can see the ball. The higher the bridge of your nose, the less you will be able to turn your head to the right and still see the ball with your right eye.

A little explanation will enable the reader to understand how important it is to see the ball with both eyes. When we look at any object, e.g. a golf ball, with both eyes (binocular vision), the image seen with one eye is superimposed 'on top of' the image seen with the other eye. That is to say, we see two separate images, and if one does not 'fit' exactly on top of the other, we are 'seeing double'. It is this superimposed image which gives the object 'body', or 'depth', or perspective.

Now if we look at the same object with one eye (monocular vision), the image appears to be flatter, or loses perspective. A golf ball would look more like a disc. It will now be apparent why we must see the ball with both eyes.

To drive the lesson home, I will relate the story of the one-eyed billiards player whose biggest 'break' was five.

He challenged a friend, who often got a break of fifty, to a match. The better player had to bandage one eye. The bet was on, and very soon the player with the bandaged eye was even missing the cue ball.

If any doubting Thomas reads this, I invite him to try it. I would back any one-eyed snooker player to beat Joe Davis with one eye bandaged. Comparably, it would be a safe bet that any one-armed sixteen handicap golfer would beat even Jack Nicklaus, if Nicklaus played with one arm.

Once again then, the rule is bend your back, then your eyes will be wide open and your head will stay down naturally, consequently you will see the ball plainly and your head will only want to turn, so that there will be only little, if any, tendency for your head to spoil the shot.

All you need do, then is to think that you 'see the ball hit'. You will probably blink, and not do so, but it doesn't matter.

USE AND MISUSE OF THE LEGS AND FEET

This calls for brief consideration of 'the set', 'the forward press', 'the pivot', 'left heel raising', 'weight transference', 'balance', 'left hip back', 'left side out of the way', 'left heel down', and 'firm left leg'.

All these movements are relatively unimportant because they happen automatically if the swing is performed as described.

The Set. This expression refers to the general set-up of the body at address, and is entirely due to the left hand being higher than the right one on the club shaft. Prove this by standing in the golfing attitude with your hands palm to palm opposite your middle. Now, keeping the left arm straight, push the right hand down until its palm is in contact with your left fingers.

What has happened? Your hands have moved to the left opposite the inside of the left leg. Weight has transferred slightly to the left. The right knee, hip, and shoulder have gone down and a little forward, while your left knee, hip, and shoulder have gone up and a little backward.

That is 'the set', and the position at impact is merely a 'live' replica of it.

The set is a naturally assumed position, and not merely a bending inwards of the right knee after assuming the stance.

The set is not so apparent in golfers who have the left hand less on top of the shaft, and who consequently play the ball nearer the middle of the stance, and usually use a flatter swing with a quicker turn of the wrists after impact. In other words the more to the left you play the ball, the more pronounced the set.

The Forward Press. The forward press is merely a slight increase of 'the set' to the left, before beginning the backswing.

It is usually said that the forward press should begin with the hands or the right knee, with which I disagree because there is a tendency to push the knee towards the ball and consequently to swing too flat and too rotatory. Also it necessitates transference of the player's attention from one part of his anatomy to another during the swing.

If you must use the forward press, do it by slightly raising the left shoulder, then you will be concentrating on the same part with which you are going to begin the backswing, and by so doing, see how your hands move straight to the left and not in a curve. By this method you will conform to my belief – which we have proved – that all movements below the chest are involuntary.

The forward press has been seen to occur by means of slow-motion photography, but nevertheless it should *not* be made a voluntary movement. A boy does it when throwing a stone but he is not aware of it.

Why become aware of it at golf? It is a natural subconscious movement which will vary in degree with different people. The natural conscious preparation to hit a golf ball – or anything else – is the backswing. Do just that, and the forward press will take care of itself, though maybe imperceptibly.

The Pivot. The pivot as usually taught is a rotation of the whole body by voluntary leg movements, which is wrong in principle, and causes swinging around, too flat.

The pivot is an inevitable accompaniment of the swing, but should be allowed to happen automatically, and not be voluntarily forced into unnatural and varying paths. In fact, the word itself, together with any thought of pivoting, should be deleted from the golfer's vocabulary – unless it be transferred to the shoulders.

Some professionals do now speak of the 'shoulder pivot', but even that designation is not correct and gives a totally wrong impression, since the shoulder movement is more complicated.

You may remember that you feel only that you push the left shoulder down, then pull it up, but that while you are doing that, both shoulders are automatically revolved (or turned) by the subconscious movement of the hips.

Left Heel Raising. The left heel should not be voluntarily raised at all. Whatever does happen will be secondary to movement elsewhere. The more upright the swing the less the heel will rise. In a correctly executed backswing the pressure should first be felt to pass to the inside edge of the left foot. Any subsequent heel raising is merely to accommodate the later stages of a full backswing and is due to the automatic turn of the hips. That is why professionals say that in short shots any left foot movement is felt rather than seen.

Weight Transference. Golf books often instruct the reader to transfer his weight to the right on the backswing, then to the left on the forward swing. This is entirely wrong, as voluntary transference of weight is bound to be carried too far.

Weight transference is involuntary and automatic with any purposeful movement of the upper part of the body, and is entirely for the purpose of subconsciously maintaining balance.

Reach to one side to pick up a book, then stop and see how your weight has transferred even without your knowledge, much less your assistance. Do the same thing again by intentionally transferring your weight with your legs, and you will probably topple over.

In the golf swing, the mere fact of swinging the club to the right or left side of the body — even though it feels to be going directly upwards — will transfer automatically exactly the amount of weight that is necessary, if you don't interfere.

Balance. Balance is very important, and is often said to be the most noticeable feature of professional golf. It will be difficult to attain if the swing is wrong, or the weight *consciously* moved from heel to toe, or for that matter in any direction.

But if the swing feels to be in a straight line, up to the right then up to the left by conscious shoulder movement as described – leaving the legs to find subconsciously their correct positions – then maintenance of balance will be simple, natural, and in fact inevitable.

Left Hip Back. To begin the forward swing by pushing the left hip backwards would necessitate transferring your attention from one part of the body to another and back again during the split-second available. Impracticable and unnecessary, as well as catastrophic!

If attempted, the whole body would revolve to the left, throwing the club across the line and causing a slice. To me this seems, and is, so obvious that I find it hard to believe that some eminent professionals advocate this method to ensure an inside-to-out swing. Don't accept anyone's statement however eminent he may be. Try it for yourself – I know what will happen – then you will start to think for yourself. I wish golfers would!

Slow-motion photography again is responsible for this fallacy, because it shows that apparently the left hip does move first; but what is overlooked is that this is a preparatory, involuntary movement, caused by the conscious movement of the upper part of the body which wields the implement. That we have proved.

Watch an expert crack a long whip across the front of his body, and you will plainly see the quick jerk of the hips to the left to be apparently the first movement, although it was probably preceded by an imperceptible shoulder movement.

But crack a whip violently yourself, and you will be conscious of using only the upper part of your body.

Therefore execute the forward swing with your left shoulder, and the left hip will go back as and when it should to maintain your balance.

Left Side Out of the Way. Golfers are told to get the left side 'out of the way' voluntarily, but this – like the left hip – will take care of itself if the swing is right. To attempt it, pulls the whole body round to the left.

Left Heel Down. Pushing the left heel down as a first move-ment is often erroneously advocated. This again is automatic, the heel being pushed down by the left hip going backwards, which in turn is due to the voluntary movement of the upper part of the body.

Firm Left Leg. This is said to be essential for a good shot, and probably is. Even if the leg is bent at impact, it must be none the less firm, though not straight.

Since the left foot when firmly on the ground becomes the fulcrum of the forward swing, it might be wondered why a good shot can sometimes be played with the left heel off the ground, or with the left knee bent at impact. The explanation is simple. The front part of the foot can be the fulcrum, the foot or leg – though 'kinked' – being held firm by contracted muscles.

The explanation of the cause of these two faults is equally simple. The left heel off the ground at impact implies too late or insufficient weight transference, due to hitting with the arms instead of first applying the body on the forward swing. The bent left knee at impact means that the swing was 'set lower down' by excessive knee bending at address.

It is not possible to transfer your thoughts from the swing to 'make' your left leg firm, then back again. In any case it is unnecessary because the left leg becomes firm automatically, by the stretching of the whole left side of the body, which is due to the left shoulder being pulled up, and the consequent backward movement of the left hip.

It will be appreciated then, that, the forward press, the 'pivot', left heel raising, weight transference, balance, left hip back, left side out of the way, left heel down, and firm left leg, are all automatic, subconscious movements, activated by simply revolving the shoulders around the horizontal upper part of the spine.

Use and Misuse of the Arms

This involves discussion of 'right elbow down', 'straight left arm', 'backswing', 'pull down with left arm', 'hitting down with irons', and 'hitting late'.

Right Elbow Down. Among the 'stars', the only one I knew of whose right elbow was allowed to go very high on the backswing was James Bruen, therefore he may be a law unto himself. At the same time I think it can be more easily explained than is usually thought. He was said to have an unusually 'high finish', therefore he must have hit definitely upwards. Also his hands were very high at the top of the backswing, in which position his right elbow would have had to go up if his backswing were excessively upright, which I suspect it was. A top of backswing photograph of him in Henry Cotton's book showed the club shaft to be well short of the horizontal despite the height of his hands. This could only mean a very firm grip and firm wrists with minimum wrist-cocking.

It seems to me that the sum total of all this is that he played golf in the same manner that I am trying to prove that most professionals do – only he did more so!

Since I am trying to show the easy road to good golf, we will not emulate Mr. Bruen's extreme though correct swing.

'Right elbow down' does not mean that it must be held consciously against the body, but merely that it should not lead the way and go upwards, which, incidentally, it will tend to do if the right hand is 'under' the shaft.

Also, it does not mean that the elbow must be perpendicularly under the shaft at the top of the backswing; which could happen only if the left wrist were well 'rolled over' on the way up. That wrist rolling is not only unnecessary but undesirable.

If the backswing is performed by the left shoulder as instructed, and maybe assisted by the left upper arm only, then all that is meant by 'right elbow down' will happen automatically, therefore it is merely another of those golf maxims which can be forgotten.

Straight Left Arm. While most professionals do maintain a straight left arm on the backswing, it is still debatable whether they would play as well if they did not. For instance the late – and great – Harry Vardon always allowed his left arm to bend on the backswing, and even deprecated a straight one. Henry Cotton said that he might emulate Vardon but found it more difficult than keeping the arm straight. Is it possible that professionals – not to mention the unfortunate amateurs – have trained themselves for years to maintain an unnaturally straight arm that is unnecessary?

Careful examination of photographs of professionals at the top of the backswing will reveal that many of them – and even some who claim to have a straight left arm – have in fact a slight bend at the elbow.

I believe that the important thing is that the left arm should be firm – which it can be only if the grip is very firm – then it will be relatively and sufficiently straight.

It seems to me that if you can maintain a straight left arm, there may be something gained, such as a definitely wide swing, and absence of the necessity to straighten the arm on the way down. But if you find it difficult, you will probably play better without it, especially if you convince yourself that it is unnecessary.

I am certain of one thing: you cannot keep the left arm straight if you swing the club back with your hand. Any use of the hand must soon bend the wrist, and the next natural thing to happen is for the elbow to bend.

That is why I am also certain that 'straight left armed' professionals do not start the backswing with the hand, even if they think, and say, they do.

I think all experts are agreed that a straight left arm at impact is essential, but there was at least one notable exception to even this rule. Mildred Zaharius, one-time woman champion of Great Britain and America, had photographs of herself in her book, *Championship Golf*, showing a bent left arm not only at the top of the backswing but also at impact, and also after impact with the elbow leading.

I am inclined to think that, as 'at the top', so 'at impact', firmness may be more important than being straight. Of course a firm straight arm has the advantage of providing a 'radius' of fixed length, whereas a firm bent arm provides a 'radius' which might vary in length.

Presuming that a straight left arm is desirable 'at the top' and 'at impact', there are four factors concerned in its production and maintenance.

(1) The player's 'build'.

(2) Firmly contracted forearm muscles.

(3) Stretching of left arm to separate wrist from shoulder.

(4) Beginning of the backswing and the forward swing by the left shoulder as instructed.

We will now consider the effects of these factors.

(1) Generally speaking, slim, 'narrow-chested' people will find it easier to maintain a straight left arm both 'at the top' and 'at impact', than fleshy broad-shouldered people.

(2) The muscles about the elbow joint are those of the forearm, which become firm when we grip anything. Therefore the more tightly we grip the club shaft the firmer these muscles will be, and the more definitely they will 'splint' the elbow joint and prevent its movement. That statement can be proved by 'doing a backswing' with the left arm, first with the hand open, and then with it tightly clenched, and noticing the different behaviour of the elbow joint.

(3) Repeat those two 'backswings' with the hand alternately open and clenched, but also stretch the arm before starting. I think you will find this helps to keep the arm straight.

(4) If you add to the above two factors beginning of a proper backswing by a downward motion of the left shoulder, you will find it much easier to keep the left arm straight. The reason for this is because the shoulder going down carries or pushes the arm from its 'top end', therefore it has no reason to bend; whereas if you started the backswing with your hand or even arm, the arm would have to drag the shoulder after it, thus

producing a further tendency to bending, in addition to that already described as due to using the hand.

After the downward moving shoulder has 'carried' the straight left arm a good way up, the upper arm may either subconsciously or consciously (you will remember) assist the action. It is the conscious use of the arm that might tend to bend it, but it must be obvious to everyone that swinging the arm by the muscles above the elbow will have less tendency to bend the elbow than by using muscles below it, i.e. those of the forearm or hand.

Regarding the straight left arm at impact, I believe that in addition to the recommended firmness of arm and grip, the most important factor is the left shoulder going upwards into its half circle groove on the forward swing, and thus 'getting out of the way', thereby leaving room for the 'long', straight left arm. The reader will remember that in effect the left arm is longer than the right one owing to the left hand being higher on the shaft. Therefore it should not be difficult to visualize that if the left shoulder was not high enough at impact, then the left elbow would have to be bent to shorten the distance between shoulder and club head, so that the club head could contact the ball.

Backswing. One need say no more about the futility of beginning the backswing with the arm than has been said under 'straight left arm'; except perhaps to remind you that to do so is making the shoulder joint the hub, which is movable, instead of the upper part of the spine which is a fixed hub which merely turns on its axis. It does not require a King Solomon to make the wise and correct choice.

Hitting Down with Irons. The word 'down' implies performing the forward swing with some portion of the arm or arms. To hit 'down' with any other part of the anatomy would involve ducking the whole body, which is exactly what many unfortunate players do, owing to this mistaken advice. We don't need to consider the consequences of this.

There is the same objection to starting the forward swing

with the arms as there is on the backswing, i.e. the movable hub, as well as all the other factors mentioned when describing the 'secret'.

I will say again that with iron clubs the ball is hit as the club head comes down, simply because impact occurs before the club head reaches the bottom of its arc, but the swing with irons is exactly the same as with woods, i.e. upwards.

Pull Down with Left Arm. This is a commonly advised wrong method of beginning the forward swing.

It is to be deprecated along with 'hitting down with irons', and for the same reasons.

Don't do it; concentrate on your left shoulder and swing upwards.

Hitting Late. Perhaps I should say a little here for the benefit of the 'arm hitters', and more later under 'hands' for the 'hand hitters'.

I will say first of all that they are both wrong. Concentrate on the left shoulder, then the arms and hands will come in automatically. There is perhaps some advantage in assisting the left shoulder by active use of the right upper arm, which is quite different from hitting late with the arms.

This so-called hitting at the correct time will occur automatically, at the correct time to suit the individual player, if the forward swing is executed mainly by the left shoulder, and is therefore rhythmical.

The term 'hitting area' – like many other golfing expressions – does more harm than good, and should be scrapped. In its place should be used the correct definition of that position in the forward swing. It should be described as the area before impact – which must vary with different players – where centrifugal force begins to increase the club head speed, and to uncock the wrists, to enable the hands and the club head to 'pass the body', and thus attain their maximum speed soon after impact.

You should be actually hitting from the very commencement of the forward swing which you begin with the left shoulder.

This body movement (initiated by the left shoulder) should be uninterruptedly completed as quickly as possible. Momentum (not you) will naturally, gradually and rhythmically increase the speed of the swing and of the club head until 'centrifugal force takes over'. But you must not interfere by some futile 'extra hitting' – either late or early – somewhere in the middle of the effort.

Think of the boy throwing a stone. Does he think of 'hitting late'? No! Does the whip-cracker think of 'hitting late'? No! Does the boxer think of 'hitting late'? No!

All these performers think of hitting from the moment they start the backswing. Their abstract thought becomes a concrete action from the moment they start the forward swing.

So it is with all similar activities, including golf.

USE AND MISUSE OF THE HANDS

This involves discussion of 'wrists and hands', 'loose grip', 'wrist-cocking', 'wrist-uncocking', 'wrist-roll', 'open face and shut face', 'scooping', 'wrist-flick', 'hitting late', 'hitting entirely with right hand', 'pull down with left hand', 'snatching', 'hands first', 'swing straight back', 'club head close to ground', and 'swaying'.

Wrists and Hands. The wrists have no strength, and no function other than to act as a hinge, therefore the wrist merely bends when the hand is used. We cannot use our wrists. The expression 'wrists of steel' is merely the nonsense of fiction. The 'strength of the wrists' is really the strength of the forearm muscles by means of which we move the hand and fingers, or grip.

Although you cannot keep your wrist firm unless you 'grip' (i.e. contract the forearm muscles), no matter how tightly you do it is still possible for your wrist to move freely. That fact – as fact it is – is contrary to the usual golf teaching that a tight grip prevents 'wrist work', and proves that I am right in claiming that no matter how tightly you grip, your wrists will function as and when they should. Prove that by clenching your right hand tightly and seeing how easily you can move your wrist.

The hands, when playing golf, merely grip or hold on to the club shaft. When that is done, they should be regarded as inseparably part of the shaft and nothing more – at any rate with all but the smallest of shots.

The muscles in the hands themselves are used chiefly for the more delicate finger work.

A good idea of wrist and hand function in the golf swing can be had by visualizing your left arm (shoulder to wrist) as a rod, and a golf club with your left hand fixed to it as another rod, your wrist being thought of as a hinge which connects the two rods together.

As the left shoulder goes down to begin the backswing, the 'wrist-hinge' will be the first part to be pushed to the right (so-called 'hands first'), then centrifugal force will gradually swing the club past the wrist (wrist-cocking). If the arm is now swung to the left by pulling the left shoulder upwards (forward swing), the club and hand will continue to go to the right thus continuing the cocking of the 'wrist-hinge'. When the wrist is fully cocked, the rebound in conjunction with centrifugal force will start the wrist-uncocking, which will be complete at impact. At this stage, therefore, the arm and the hand attached to the club, will be in one straight line.

Combined with the wrist-cocking and uncocking, is a slight wrist roll (so-called), which can be appreciated by visualizing the arm being slightly rolled or twisted to the right during the backswing, and to the left during the forward swing.

The 'reverse wrist-cocking' and 'wrist-roll' after impact, are not apparent for some distance, owing to the fact that the arm, as well as the hand and club, is moving quickly onwards.

It will now be apparent that the hands merely hold the club, and that to obtain rhythm and good timing, the wrist-cocking, wrist-uncocking, and wrist-roll must all be automatic and sub-conscious, and entirely the result of momentum and centrifugal force.

Loose Grip. Varying degrees of gripping with different fingers, and with either hand, as often advocated, I am sure are not only unnecessary but undesirable. Latterly quite a number of professionals have advised a firmer grip, some with the left hand, some with both.

In my opinion, 'holding on' at the top of the backswing, and firm contact with the ball at impact (both acknowledged to be essential), are only possible if the grip with all parts of both hands is very firm. This will not interfere with necessary wrist work.

Wrist-cocking. This, like other wrist movements, will occur automatically and to the varying extent necessary for different lengths of shot, no matter how tightly you grip the club, providing you concentrate on your left shoulder and do not attempt to interfere by using your hands.

The cocking is entirely subconscious, and is due to the momentum caused by the push back of the club developing into a swing, plus centrifugal force.

Actually, it is probably best to forget all about wrist-cocking, by gripping the club firmly and feeling, at the top of the swing, as though the wrists had not cocked. They will, despite your belief that you have prevented it, whereas if you try consciously to do it with your hands you are sure to relax your grip, over-swing, bend your left elbow and probably lose control of the club.

Most high handicap players swing farther back than they think they do. Ask a friend to watch you do a full swing, grip firmly and decide to finish the backswing with the club pointing to the sky. You will find that usually, in these circumstances, the club shaft goes nearer the correct horizontal than – as you thought – the 'perpendicular'. The difference between your sensation and the fact, is due to your inability to appreciate by means of your hands the effect of the momentum of the swing on the club head.

It is surprising how small an amount of wrist-cocking is possible in the average wrist. Address a ball, then without permitting any movement above the wrists, raise the club head towards your face with your hands only. You will probably find that the left index 'finger knuckle' moves about one inch only, while the club head travels two or three feet – and that is without momentum!

It is that 'one inch' that deceives you; therefore feel that it has not happened, then momentum will not only do it for you, but will make it act as a powerful spring from which to rebound automatically on the forward swing.

Wrist-uncocking. All that has been said about wrist-cocking applies even more to wrist-uncocking. That is because there was no wound-up spring to begin the backswing and wrist-cocking, which there is for the forward swing and wrist-uncocking. Also there is infinitely more momentum on the forward swing.

Uncocking of your wrists will occur automatically – and also of your left elbow – at the right time and place, so long as you concentrate on your left shoulder traversing its groove, maintain a really firm grip with all parts of both hands, and don't interfere by trying to use your hands.

Wrist-roll. The first thing to say about this is that it has nothing at all to do with the wrists. It is the twisting of the forearms which changes our hands from palm down to palm up. Also – during a golf swing – there is a slight twist of the *upper* arm, without which the right elbow would not remain 'low down'. Although wrist-roll is performed by the arms, I am discussing it in this section because it is usually – though mistakenly – associated with the hands.

There should be no conscious wrist-roll either on the backswing or on the forward swing. This belief appears to be at variance with the statement by some professionals, that at or about impact the right hand turns sharply over the left; but what they don't explain is that this movement is 'absorbed' into the rapid onward movement of the arms and hands, and therefore is not apparent until later in the swing.

The fact is that the right hand crossing over the left is

greatly an illusion, due to the simultaneous alteration in the position of the arms. Before impact the right elbow is much nearer the body, that is, farther 'back' than the left one, whereas after impact the left one becomes farther 'back'.

Undoubtedly there is some wrist-roll in the golf swing, though it is only slight, and entirely due to momentum. It will occur as and when it should automatically if you don't interfere by attempting to do it voluntarily.

Wrist-cocking and wrist-rolling as well as wrist-uncocking and wrist-unrolling, are combined movements; and to try consciously to improve on nature, by increasing one or the other, is comparable to putting the proverbial spanner in the works.

Open Face and Shut Face. There is definitely room for some clarification of this subject, especially with regard to the position at the top of the backswing.

Beyond stating that at the top of the backswing when the club face faces 'front' the club face is open, and when it faces the sky it is shut, most professionals fight shy of the subject. I disagree with these definitions, and believe that in both instances the face is open, the difference being one of degree. I will go further and say that a shut faced position of the club at the top of a golf swing is a physical impossibility. The nearest approach to it was the swing of James Bruen, who carried his right elbow very high in the backswing, but even so, by means of a loop his forward swing became more orthodox.

Let us see what opens and shuts the club face.

Address a ball, then, without any wrist-roll, make the club head describe a quarter circle, on the ground, around your right leg. Now although the club shaft points to your right, and the club face faces directly forwards, it has not opened, because your arms, hands and the club head still have the same relationship as at the address.

Again address the ball, then without swinging, open, then shut, the club face. You had to 'roll' your wrists to the right to open the face, and to the left to shut it. Remember that during the golf swing it is involuntary wrist-roll that opens and shuts the club face.

Of course, I know that if it were possible, from the address position, to carry the club head to the top with its face at right angles to the target line all the way, that the face would then face the sky, and that would be an extreme 'shut face swing'. But that is a physical impossibility and therefore proves nothing.

Will the reader attempt that swing now. He will find that he can get his hands only about shoulder-high, and that the club must remain in front of him; also – and this is important – his wrists have rolled to the left and the back of his left hand faces the ground. But, on any backswing that is physically possible, even before the hands are shoulder-high, and even in the so-called shut-faced swing which makes the club face at the top face the sky, the back of the left hand faces mainly to the sky.

Surely that is proof of wrist-roll to the right and a consequent open face!

I am sure there has been too much made of the difference between the 'English open-faced swing' and the so-called 'New American shut-faced swing', which as I have shown are both 'open-faced', the difference being only one of degree.

Almost all photographs of experts – American and British – half-way through the backswing show, as above described, the club head pointing 'backwards', and the club face partly facing the sky. The degree varies with different people, as also does the level at which the face opening begins; e.g. if the club head 'moves last', the wrist-roll and face-opening will be thereby delayed.

At least one of the modern notable American so-called shut-face-swing school – whose photographs show what I have just described – says that on the backswing the club face neither shuts nor opens. Other people say it shuts; I have just *proved* that it opens. We must not always accept expert opinions in golf or in anything. They often differ and are often wrong.

From that half-way position to the top of the backswing, the toe of the club head leads, and ultimately swings towards your back, stopping with the club face in some degree facing the sky.

Now, this club face position at the top has nothing at all to do with the so-called open-faced or shut-faced swinging. The degree to which it faces the sky is influenced by the grip, i.e. the more the left hand is on top of the shaft, the more the club face faces the sky. But the real factor is the position of the hands at the top of the backswing. The farther 'back' the hands, the more the club face faces the sky. This can be seen by comparing professionals' photographs. In addition, the farther back the hands, the more the right wrist – and elbow – are under the shaft. Note this well: that is *why* the left hand is more in front of the shaft and with less wrist-cock.

This 'far back' position of the hands may be influenced by long arms, but the chief factor in permitting it is a low left shoulder – as previously described – at the top of the backswing. The player must not attempt to push his hands backwards; they go into that position automatically as he pushes his left shoulder down and his left upper arm up.

If the reader will put himself into the top of the swing position just described, and then deliberately cock his left wrist more – watching it – he will see the back of his left hand to some extent comes towards the back of his forearm, which movement will cause the club face to face less to the sky.

He may find it difficult to cock the left wrist more unless he brings his hands a little 'forward'. This apparently small fact provides the key to those cases in which the club face at the top of the swing is facing forwards. The club face is in that position, and the 'toe' pointing to the ground, when the hands are less far 'back', so that the club shaft is more above the shoulder, i.e. nearer the neck. In addition, in these cases, the right elbow is usually a little backwards and higher, whereas the left wrist is more under the shaft, and with more cocking and a longer backswing.

That is the real and only difference between the so-called shut-faced and open-faced positions at the top. Briefly, when the hands are well 'back', the left wrist is more to the 'front', and there is less left wrist-cocking, therefore the club face in some degree faces the sky; whereas, when the hands are less far back, the left wrist is more under the shaft, there is more left wrist-cocking, therefore the club face faces the front. This explanation accounts for all the intermediate positions of the club face with different players.

Notable examples of the top of the swing position with the club face facing the front (and hands 'less far back') were Bobby Jones, Leonard Crawley, and Percy Alliss in his younger days. (This can be seen from photographs taken at the time.)

This brings us to the conclusion that there is no such thing as a correct open-faced swing or correct shut-faced swing, because the former would require voluntary wrist-roll, while the latter would require voluntary inhibition of the natural automatic wrist-roll – both incorrect because wrist-roll should be involuntary.

If the backswing is performed as described, the correct position at the top will be inevitable, then when the forward swing is begun by pulling the left shoulder upwards, the club head when about half-way down will be in some degree 'behind' the player, while the 'toe' will be in some degree pointing backwards, and the club face in some degree facing the sky. This position of the club head and club face is proof that the club face is still open.

Again as on the backswing, this position of the club head and face on the forward swing, can be seen in photographs of most British or American experts.

From this position, the continued upward movement of the left shoulder into its half circle groove will carry the club face 'square to the line' at impact and for a considerable distance beyond, because the 'reverse wrist-roll' is delayed.

The 'after-impact' position of the club face is further discussed in the next section.

Scooping. Professionals always say 'don't scoop'. Scooping, as I understand it, is striking the ball and allowing the club head to follow it with the face square to the target, but at the same time leaving the hands behind at impact position; or worse still, raising the hands as though to lift – instead of loft – the ball.

That, of course, is bad, but there is nothing wrong with the club head position if the hands also travel onwards. Indeed it is very desirable and is proof that the shot has been hit upwards, since in many cases it has the effect of bending the back of the left hand towards the forearm. This hinge-like bending of the left wrist is plainly shown in many photographs of first-class golfers, both with short and long clubs.

That square club face for a considerable distance after impact – with or without the left wrist hingeing – is the natural conse- quence of the swing which I advocate, and is typical of the so- called American shut-faced swing, as well as of the swings of many British experts; thus bearing out my belief that the difference between the British and American swings is merely one of degree.

The possibility of the above described hinge-like action of the left wrist, renders wristwork even more complicated; and suggests that the player who tries to find the combination of wrist-uncocking, wrist-rolling, and wrist-hingeing, to 'suit him', is making a grave mistake.

I think, providing the swing is executed correctly and always the same, the right combination of these wrist actions for the individual player will occur automatically, and will depend chiefly on whether the swing tends to be upright or flat. The flatter the swing the more the wrist-roll. The more upright the swing the more the hinge movement – or no wrist movement at all, until the wrist-roll becomes apparent later.

Since my thesis is based on a horizontal upper part of the spine producing an upright swing, I must plump for no wrist movement at all soon after impact, unless it be a little hinge-like action.

Wrist-flick. This is really the same as wrist-roll and is some- times referred to as the 'flick at the bottom' of the swing.

It is a dangerous conception, as it encourages a quick open- ing and shutting of the club face by the hands, with as many possible directions for the ball to travel as there are tangents to a circle. It is another expression and idea best forgotten.

Maybe instead of the flick being achieved by a wrist-roll, a wrist-hingeing is advocated as mentioned under 'scooping'. Any method of flicking with the hands should be taboo, as their function is merely to grip the club. The only flick that is necessary is the subconscious uncocking of the wrists.

Hitting Late. As with the arms, hitting late with the hands implies making an extra effort in the middle of the forward swing. Could anything be more calculated to upset rhythm?

Again, hitting late with the hands envisages a voluntary uncocking of the wrists partway down, but wrist-uncocking should be involuntary and the automatic result of the rebound from wrist-cocking, which is not complete until the forward swing is under way.

Therefore, with a correct swing induced by the left shoulder, all that is implied by the misleading expression 'hitting late', will occur automatically.

You should feel that you are hitting from the start of the forward swing, i.e. early!

Hitting Entirely with the Right Hand. At least one expert advocates doing this when playing a full shot. It seems to me – and it has been my experience when trying the method – that a full shot played entirely right-handed holds the weight back, with obvious undesirable consequences.

I also feel that those who think they do this, have so well trained the left side of the body, that it functions without their knowledge.

I have already discussed the possibility of right-handed play with short shots, but even with these, starting with the left side appears to be desirable, to ensure the rhythmic flow of whatever weight should go into the shot.

Lastly, I would condemn hitting with the right hand just as I would the left hand, because the function of both hands is only to grip.

The hit is assisted by the right upper arm, not hand.

Pull Down with the Left Hand. What I have said about pulling down with the left arm also applies to the hand – only more so.

It is pulling on the 'middle of the rope'. Also it must start to undo the wrist-cocking, since you cannot use your hand without wrist movement in the same direction.

Even worse, you will be undoing the wrist-cocking before it is complete, since the wrist should be still in process of cocking after the forward swing has well begun.

Lastly, to think of the hand at all, is more likely than anything else to cause snatching. Therefore forget it.

Snatching. I believe that much the commonest cause of this is pulling down with the left hand or arm. The only other possible cause is anxiety to hit the ball, and this will not cause snatching if the forward swing is commenced with the left shoulder.

Hands First. The conception of this is correct only in so far as the hands should begin to move before the club head, although the 'start' may be so slight as to be almost imperceptible. That is the reason why some say hands before club head while others say both together. The important thing is that there should be no wrist-cocking at this stage.

But the left hand should not be the first part of the anatomy to move. The left shoulder going down pushes the left arm to the right, causing the wrist to bend slightly 'backwards' and move to the right, before the hand.

To perform 'hands first' by means of the hand or hands, would tend to make the shoulder, and therefore the head, also move to the right, i.e. to sway. These are natural consequential movements to be expected in such circumstances.

Think only of the left shoulder, and the hand and the club head will move correctly.

Swing Straight Back. The experts often say 'start the backswing by swinging the club head straight back'. They variously say 'on the reverse target line', 'for first few inches', 'six to eight inches', 'about a foot', or 'a foot or so'.

Deliberately attempting to do any of these distances will tend to make you look to see if it is happening, and also to make the whole body sway to the right.

Actually, the flatter the swing, and consequently the more inclined the plane of the *club head* arc, the shorter will be the distance that the club head remains on that straight line. Conversely, the more upright the swing, the more upright the plane of the club head arc, and therefore the longer will the club head travel straight behind the ball.

But, as previously stated, by starting the backswing by depressing the left shoulder, and feeling that you are swinging the club head straight up, it will automatically go straight back behind the ball for the necessary distance.

In this instance again, people confuse what they should do, with what happens in consequence of doing something else.

Club Head Close to the Ground. In conjunction with 'straight back', goes the instruction to keep the club head close to the ground. Both have the same consequences, as described; also, both tend to keep the left shoulder high and to restrict the shoulder pivot.

Particularly is this the case with 'club head close to the ground', because the player – being uncertain when to let it come up – may let the club head swing round his right leg like a scythe. Perhaps that fault may be partly corrected during the course of the swing if it always happened the same. But – and this is important – it would never be twice the same, therefore the backswing would vary, especially with different clubs, and would never get into anything approaching a 'groove'.

Once again then, 'left shoulder down' will not only ensure the club head going straight back, but straight back close to the ground – and automatically for the correct distance.

Swaying. Embryo golfers are always told not to sway – and rightly so – but how can they avoid it if they are also told to do the aforementioned things which cause it?

'Swaying' implies a lateral movement of the head alternately to right and left. It is important to realize that this is a perfectly natural movement when playing a shot, visualized as a backswing straight to the right and a hit straight to the left.

Take the example of a tennis player: as he swings back in preparation for, say, a forehand drive, his head moves to the right with the rest of his body, then to the left as he strikes.

That is where golf appears to be unnatural, but it becomes natural enough if you do an upright swing by revolving the shoulders around a horizontal upper part of the spine, and thus keep the head – like a turnip on a spike – in the same position during the entire swing, until the ball has been dispatched.

That is why I maintain that the feel of the swing, as distinct from what happens automatically, should be merely up to the right and up to the left.

I would again stress the fact that the head not only can, but should, turn right or left, on its own axis, as much as it – or its owner – likes.

Use and Misuse of the Fairway

This involves a study of 'divots' and 'ball position', and since they are inseparable they will be considered together.

Divots and Ball Position. Divots are of two kinds, intentional and unintentional. The former are usually considered desirable, and are taken in front of the ball after it has been hit; the latter are definitely undesirable, and are taken behind the ball before it has been hit.

The length and depth of any divot depends on how far behind the bottom of its arc, the club head contacts the ground, whereas if the club head contacts the ground exactly at the bottom of its arc, there will be no divot. For our present purposes we can ignore any flattening of the bottom of the arc.

What happens to the ball will depend on whether it is in front of, at, or behind the bottom of the arc. See diagram No. 13, in which the letters mark the sections of the diagram as well as the club shaft, while the arrows indicate the direction of the forward swing.

'A' represents a clean shot with no divot, the hands being above the ball, which is the normal position at the bottom of the swing arc.

'B' represents an intentional small shallow divot, the hands being slightly ahead of the ball, which is therefore to the right. The ground was struck in front of, i.e. after, the ball.

'C' represents an intentional large deep divot, the hands being well ahead of the ball, which is therefore still nearer the right foot. Again the ground was struck in front of, i.e. after, the ball.

'D' represents an unintentional divot caused by the hands being too near the ball, and due to either standing too near the ball, or using a club which is too long. In either case the ground is struck behind, i.e. before, the ball. Incidentally being too near the ball is probably also the commonest cause of 'shanking', i.e. hitting the ball with the neck of the club.

'E' represents an unintentional divot, the ball being in the normal no-divot position, with the hands above it at address. This divot is due to some fault keeping the weight back on the right leg, and consequently also keeping the hands and the arc back, so that the ground is struck behind, i.e. before, the ball, which is topped.

'F' represents an intentional divot, the hands being ahead of the ball which is nearer the right foot, and in a 'cuppy lie', i.e. it is partly under the ground. Theoretically, the ball should always be struck before the ground, but when the ball is partly submerged, it might require too steep a blow to dislodge it, necessitating the ball lying even to the right of the right foot. In this case, it seems to me to be geometrically correct to play the ball only reasonably far to the right of the stance, and to take a small divot before the ball, and a larger one after it. This would be similar to a semi-explosion shot from sand, since – you must remember – that if the ball is stuck in the earth, the earth must be soft. This is the only instance when a divot must be taken, and don't forget to grip very firmly.

We must now consider what advantages there are, if any, in taking a divot with a straightforward iron shot.

To do so is generally supposed to make a ball fly straight and more true, and probably farther. It will undoubtedly – other things being equal – make the ball go farther, because by playing the ball farther to the right you are, in effect, converting the club to one of higher power. That is to say, a five would be equal to a four or even a three, because as you ground the club head farther to the right its face becomes nearer the vertical. But there is no advantage in this, as, if you require more distance you can use a more powerful club and play the ball from the normal no-divot position.

Regarding the ball flying more truly and the vaunted advantage of 'squeezing' the ball between the club head and the earth, I have grave doubts. See diagram No. 14, in which:

'A' represents the face of a number nine striking the ball with no divot.

'B' represents the face of a number nine converted to a number seven by playing the ball nearer the right foot, with the intention of taking a shallow divot.

'C' represents the face of a number nine converted to a number five by playing the ball still nearer the right foot, with the intention of taking a large divot.

Now study the diagram and see if you can detect any difference in these three applications to the ball. As I see it, 'A', 'B', and 'C' are all approximately tangents to a circle (the ball), and if the diagram be turned round you can convert any one into either of the others. Further, as they all strike the ball at the same angle, they will produce an equal amount of backspin. Wherein then is the advantage of the divot-taking blows over the other?

I cannot see any. In fact, the 'lower' the ball is struck – as with no divot – the greater will be the forward propulsion, which is – I think – the primary object.

A very fair simile can be found in playing billiards, viz. it is equally possible to put 'stop', 'bottom', or backspin on the ball whether you strike it horizontally or almost vertically, but the billiard ball will travel farther if struck horizontally – which is comparable to 'no divot'.

So much for the 'advantages' of taking a divot! What are the disadvantages? Briefly, the shot is made more difficult, more complicated, more varied, and less foolproof, as follows:

(1) Playing the ball nearer the right foot necessitates adjustment of the grip.

(2) The shaft will not be at right angles to the intended flight of the ball.

(3) Standing a shade nearer the ball to allow for the bottom of the arc being 'under the earth'.

(4) A slight increase of body bending to lower the hands.

(5) A tighter grip to counteract contact with the earth.

(6) A likelihood of the club shaft turning in the hands at impact and causing a foul shot.

(7) Because the ball is farther to the right the shot feels different, and also looks different since you may be looking more at the front of the ball.

(8) For the reasons in No. 7, you may hold the weight to the left, or transfer too far to the right.

(9) The human element of error may produce slight differences of contact with the ball, and consequently divots of different sizes and of different resistances to the blow.

(10) The resistance will further differ with the condition of the ground, which may be harder or softer even on the same course and therefore during the course of one round.

I am forced to the conclusion – and it has been my experience – that it is much easier, more consistent, and no disadvantage to play straightforward iron shots with the ball in the normal no-divot position at the bottom of the arc.

Admittedly, most professionals take divots, but some, notably the late Harry Vardon – than whom there has probably never been a better golfer – have thought them unnecessary. What proved better for these great players will surely prove better for many lesser players; and is it not possible that many professionals have slavishly accepted and followed the divot-taking dictum of others without proving its advantages – or otherwise?

However, each player should find for himself which method suits him better, and then, except in exceptional circumstances, stick to it.

One final word about divots: if you must take them, replace them.

CHAPTER 5

CO-ORDINATION OF THE THREE
FACTORS – WITH OTHER DETAILS

Shape of the Body.
Feel of the Swing.
Backswing.
Forward Swing.
Postscript.
Quintessence.

SHAPE OF THE BODY

REGARDING the shape of your spine – and consequently of course – your back, always have the upper part of it about horizontal; and feel that you are facing the top of the ball, that it is under the upper part of your body rather than in front of you, and that you are looking down at it with wide open eyes.

With the ball somewhere opposite the left half of your body, you will then be looking, as you should be, at the 'top back' of it.

Your back has to be bent the appropriate amount, until the club head rests on the ground. Do not make the mistake of applying the club head to the ground by 'increasing' the angle which your hands, and therefore also the club shaft, make with your arms. (Do not misunderstand what is meant by 'increasing the angle'. The angle is increased when it is less apparent, because then the arms and the club shaft are more nearly in a straight line.)

You can guard against that by remembering that your arms should be hanging straight down, i.e. perpendicularly, at least with the short and medium length clubs. Even with the long clubs the arms should be almost perpendicular, the hands being only slightly more forward than the shoulders, and never 'reaching forward'.

Think of your head as being not above your shoulders, but in front of them and facing downwards; and think of your shoulders and arms as being 'in front' of your legs. Don't think of an upright body with arms and club sticking forwards.

Those are the details of the forward curve of the body, but remember that there is also a lateral curve to the left. Remember that that is due entirely to the right hand being lower than the left one on the shaft of the club.

If you play the ball opposite the left half of your body, which this hand position demands, then you will assume that shape, or 'set', of the body quite naturally. You must not try any tricks such as 'placing' your left shoulder or right knee. If you do so you will overdo the lateral curve.

FEEL OF THE SWING

So far as your conscious feelings are concerned, always visualize the golf swing – back and forward – as essentially an almost perpendicular revolving of the shoulders around an almost horizontal upper part of the spine.

That is simplicity itself, and if you remember it you cannot go far wrong.

Standing erect, when the upper part of the spine is of course practically perpendicular, a 'golf swing' would be around the body, but the club head 'at impact' would be two or three feet above the ground. But when the back is correctly bent so that the upper part of the spine is practically horizontal, although you still swing identically around the upper part of the spine, the feeling in, and the effects upon, all that part of the body below the chest is entirely different.

In the former case the feeling was entirely of rotation and swinging in a consequent flat circle. In the latter case, the feeling was of a left to right, then right to left movement, and of swinging in a consequent 'straight' line, more or less.

In actual fact it becomes almost a 'perpendicular circle', in other words, an upright swing. Even in this latter event there is a rotation of the lower part of the body, but it is secondary to what you do with your shoulders, and therefore it is not impressed on your consciousness, i.e. it is a subconscious movement.

There is a subtle difference between these two swings. When you swing rotatorily, or flat, the whole body is moving in the same direction, therefore there is no check, or brake, at the top of the backswing, and consequently you tend to lose your balance. On the other hand, when you rotate the upper part of your body vertically around a horizontal axis (the upper part of the spine), this causes the lower part of the body, after a slight lateral shift, to rotate horizontally around a more or less vertical axis (the lower part of the spine).

It is the fact that these two rotations – one voluntary and vertical, the other involuntary and horizontal – act as a check, or brake, on each other near their completion, that renders the very important balance not only automatic but inevitable.

As the shoulders are revolved around the upper part of the spine during the execution of the backswing, the left arm and the club go up, and also back. I would stress that this backward movement is not deliberate; in fact, it is an illusion. This illusion is entirely due to the subconscious turning of the lower part of the body carrying the shoulders and the club round to the right. The feeling was merely 'left shoulder down and left upper arm up'. At the top of the backswing, the left arm is still – as it must be – 'in front' of the upper part of the body.

Exactly the same thing occurs, and feeling is experienced, on the forward swing after impact.

BACKSWING

The backswing is commenced by pushing the left shoulder down, which has the effect of setting the hub of the swing (the upper part of the spine) in motion. At the same time or immediately afterwards, the left hand with the club is pushed upwards by the left shoulder muscles acting on the upper arm. The push soon changes to a swing.

These two movements occur simultaneously or practically so, and are complementary. That is to say, each helps the other. The shoulder going down helps the arm and the club to go up; and the arm going up ensures the shoulder going well down and then to the right. These combined movements also ensure a full shoulder pivot, and the hands holding the club being well 'back', in line with the tip of the right shoulder, at the top of the backswing.

While you have in the above simple manner executed a perfect backswing, many other things have occurred automatically.

(1) You thought only of the left side, but the right arm assumed its natural and correct position. The right upper arm remained near your body until late in the swing, then if the swing were long enough to need it, it was involuntarily 'lifted' off your body by the swing, the elbow still pointing more or less downwards.

(2) As the left shoulder went down, the right one went up, and the hands travelled to the right on the same level as at the address: consequently for the first foot or so the club head travelled straight back to the right close to the ground.

(3) As the shoulders gradually turned, ultimately to make the chest face to the right, so the arms and the club were carried round, and appeared to swing on an inclined plane. This shoulder turning you will remember was due to the automatic rotation of the 'pedestal' or lower part of the body. The 'inclined plane illusion' was augmented by the subconscious arm twisting to the right, which occurred in conjunction with the similarly subconscious wrist-cocking.

At this point I had better admit the obvious; that even with an upright swing as described, the club head (note well, I said club 'head' and not your hands) does swing on an inclined plane, but that is no concern of the player's!

His sensation is of swinging his arms, more or less in a straight line. That is why I call it an 'inclined plane illusion'. Your sensations and feelings are entirely in your own body, and not in the wood and steel of the club.

Of course you can always tell, by the position of your hands, the place and angle of the club head; but the professionals' admonition, 'to be aware of the position of the club head', has a lot to answer for.

(4) When approaching the top of the backswing, the club face having been gradually opened by the slight, natural, involuntary twisting of the forearms to the right, the club shaft was pointing backwards and to the sky in a line parallel to the club shaft at address position.

Here again, you must not *swing* into that position. It occurs automatically owing to the involuntary rotation of the 'pedestal', and the involuntary forearm twist which also cause the back of the left hand to face somewhat to the sky.

(5) When the shoulders had completed their 'pivot' the hands would be in line with the right shoulder, over which the club shaft would shortly be pointing to the target, by which time the wrists would have almost completed their automatic cocking.

(6) Your weight had transferred exactly as much as it should without any conscious help from you.

(7) In the meantime, the right hip had gone backwards, and the left one forwards; the left knee bending, and the left foot rolling on to its inside edge with a tendency for the heel to rise.

You have now completed the backswing – what little you had to do – and all the subconscious occurrences have happened. Your head is in its original position slightly turned to the right, or has been turned there by the late stages of the shoulder pivot; you are looking down at the 'top back of the ball'; you feel perfectly balanced; you are ready to begin the forward swing while the wrists are still cocking.

Forward Swing

Briefly, on any full shot your thoughts from the very beginning of the forward swing should be of speed and of hitting upwards 'with all you've got'; remembering to maintain a firm grip with all parts of both hands and to 'see the ball hit'.

Soon after 'thinking' you have seen the ball hit, your shoulders will twist your neck and compel your head to turn to the left.

You will have exactly the same sensations with the irons as with the woods, and also even with an explosion shot from a bunker. The iron shots will be downward hits even though you are hitting upwards, because the ball – being farther to the right – will be contacted by the club head as it comes down, and before it has reached, or at any rate passed, the bottom of the arc. We have already discussed the disastrous consequences of really hitting down.

The first and most important thing to think of – in fact maybe the only thing – is the left shoulder, which you pull up as quickly as you can, the moment it has momentarily stopped on completion of *its* backswing. You will remember that at that moment the remainder of the back swing (of arm, hand and club head) is not quite complete.

In performing its half circle, the left shoulder must first go to the left, then up, and finally to the right behind your neck; but the upward movement is the one that is apt to be forgotten, and at the same time is the most important, because it ensures the left shoulder being high, and both shoulders being square to the line, at impact, instead of turned to the left.

While the left shoulder is leading the forward swing into 'the groove', several things happen automatically without any assistance from the player.

(1) Your weight is transferred to the left.

(2) Your left hip goes backwards 'out of the way'.

(3) Your left foot goes flat on to the ground, and the left leg becomes firm.

(4) Your arms, with the wrists now fully cocked, and the club head trailing behind, are involuntarily brought down in their correct relative positions (i.e. right elbow close to your body, and the left arm farther away from you) into the – so-called – hitting area, thus ensuring the normal inside-to-out swing.

(5) In a flash, the wrists involuntarily uncock, and the club head makes 'solid contact' with the ball which travels straight 'down the middle'. Meanwhile, the hands travel straight on without stopping, and so quickly that the 'crossing over' of the hands (reverse 'wrist-roll') appears to be delayed until well into the – so-called – follow through.

(6) The back-bending and the intention to hit upwards prevents the head from being pulled up, but when the right shoulder is nearly 'under the chin' your twisted neck turns your head to the left.

(7) The momentum from hitting upwards ensures the club head following the ball, and travelling its fastest after impact – which most experts agree, it should. This also makes what is mistakenly called 'hitting late' inevitable though involuntary. Also a full 'follow through' and a 'high finish' are ensured, since you actually hit into them.

(8) Meanwhile, the right hip automatically came forward, causing the right foot to roll on to its inside edge and finally more or less on to its 'toe' as the entire weight moved on to the firm left leg.

You have now completed the forward swing – what little you had to do – and all the subconscious occurrences have happened.

Now while a thoroughly efficient forward swing can be performed by thinking only of the left shoulder as above described, it would be fatuous of me to suggest that your very powerful shoulder muscles cannot assist the shot by swinging the upper arms.

With the intention to hit upwards, I am convinced that these muscles will function to some extent automatically; and what is more, at the right time and place, since you cannot hit upwards with your arms until they have come down into the accepted 'hitting area'. Remember that they come down that far automatically in consequence of the body movement initiated by the left shoulder, so that by the time your 'thought of hitting' is transformed into 'action', you are in a position to hit upwards.

Therefore I would suggest, that after you have mastered what we will call the 'left-shoulder-up' forward swing, you then try voluntarily to assist it by swinging your upper arms with your shoulder muscles.

If you can 'time' this action correctly, you should gain extra length.

With the intention to hit upwards 'with all you've got' firmly in your mind, begin the forward swing by pulling your left shoulder upwards as quickly as possible.

Immediately that movement has started, hit upwards with your right upper arm (not your hand), leaving the left shoulder muscles to come into the shot automatically – which they will do because your mind is already on your left shoulder.

With practice you may acquire the feeling of the left shoulder and the right arm, as above described beginning the forward swing simultaneously. But if you try too soon to do it that way, you may find that sometimes the right arm will 'get in first', before the left shoulder has determined the groove. In that case you would probably not transfer your weight properly to the left, and in consequence have both heels off the ground at impact, or worse – 'take a divot' before contacting the ball, or worse still – top the ball or miss it altogether.

Never forget that it is the left shoulder going upwards that produces the desirable grooved swing. Nothing must supersede that.

When using the right arm in the manner described, I know that some people will feel that they are hitting with their right forearm or hand, but I am certain that it is the upper arm – activated by the powerful shoulder muscles – that should be thought of and cultivated in hitting the ball, because that method, by swinging the whole arm correctly from its top end, keeps the arm straight, thus ensuring a wide swing. The action could be likened to the boxer's 'straight left' from the shoulder.

POSTSCRIPT

To avoid any possibility of misunderstanding we will examine three important items – metaphorically – under the microscope.

(1) I have repeatedly stated that a golf shot should be a straight line shot, and emphasized that the left shoulder and the hands feel to be travelling in a straight line. That is to say, the left shoulder goes straight down then straight up; and the hands go straight up to the right then straight up to the left.

I used that expression deliberately, to get away from the idea of swinging around the whole body. But you do swing around the upper part of the body, therefore it is obvious that the degree of 'straightness' of the swing will vary with the degree of back-bending. The nearer the upper part of the spine is to the horizontal, the more upright will be the swing and the 'straighter' the feeling of the shoulder and hand arcs.

(2) The most important movement in the whole golf swing is that which begins the backswing, therefore it is desirable to have some means of checking its accuracy.

With the best intentions in the world to begin by revolving the shoulders around the upper part of the spine, it is very easy to think you are doing so while in fact you are revolving your body around the lower part of the spine.

The best way to judge the correctness or otherwise of the backswing, is by the nature of the forward swing after impact. That is what professionals mean when they say that a good follow through and a high finish cannot influence the ball after it has gone, but that it is proof of the correctness of what happened before impact.

Having completed a swing, if you had the feeling after impact of hitting upwards and then going to the left over your left shoulder, then the downward movement of the left shoulder on the backswing was correct. But if you felt that the forward swing after impact turned too much to the left, i.e. too early, and consequently around any part of your body below the left shoulder, and therefore not sufficiently upwards, that was because your left shoulder was not high enough at, and after, impact.

The reason the left shoulder was not high enough, was because it did not go down perpendicularly enough on the backswing. Therefore repeat the swing until you get sufficient 'down-ness' on the backswing, to produce sufficient 'up-ness' on the forward swing.

I will anticipate criticism and agree that it would be reasonable to think that if you turned the left shoulder forwards towards the ball, that the hands and the club shaft would finish farther 'back' than if you pushed the shoulder downwards. Reasonable though it may seem it is quite wrong.

If you turn the shoulder towards the ball, the left heel will come up too far, balance will be insecure, therefore the shoulder pivot will be incomplete, and at the top of the backswing the club shaft will probably be above your neck and pointing to the left of the target.

Conversely, if you push the left shoulder straight down, the left foot will roll on to its inside edge, the heel rising but slightly, your balance will be good, you will get a full shoulder pivot, and at the top of the backswing the club shaft will be above the tip of your right shoulder – or even farther back – and pointing to the target.

Compare those two shoulder movements – don't take my word for it!

(3) I have discussed the part which the arms play in the golf swing, and admitted the possibility of their voluntary use. All the same, I believe that a majority of golfers will get better results – except maybe in the short shots – if they forget all about their arms (except to grip firmly), and concentrate entirely on the left shoulder; but remember to move it through a full half circle to behind the neck.

It is that *quick half circle* that gives power and length.

In this event, don't imagine that your arms, through your shoulder muscles, are doing nothing. They will probably do more subconsciously, and certainly with more accurate timing, than you could do with them consciously.

I will again anticipate criticism by saying that it is because so much of the golf swing is automatic, that golf professionals hold such divergent views as to whether golf is a right or a left-handed game – or both.

For the same reason, their views are no less divergent on the subject of which part of the anatomy starts and continues both the backswing and the forward swing.

It is because professionals have overlooked the fact that most of the details of the golf swing are subconsciously performed, that they are unable to analyse it accurately or with any degree of unanimity.

QUINTESSENCE

Apart from maintaining a firm grip, there are only four anatomical parts with which we are consciously concerned in executing the golf swing. They are the upper part of the spine, the left 'shoulder', and the left and right UPPER arms.

The first is used in PREPARATION for the swing; the third and fourth can be left to themselves; the second is indispensable.

Therefore the LEFT SHOULDER is our sheet anchor.

Whatever we forget, we must remember what to do with the left shoulder.

By this means we find ourselves with ONE point of concentration for the execution of the entire golf swing; and also with the knowledge that we will 'SWING IN THE GROOVE'.

THAT – in a nutshell – is 'THE GOLF SECRET'.

INDEX

125

OUR PUBLISHING POLICY

HOW WE CHOOSE

Our policy is to consider every deserving manuscript and we can give special editorial help where an author is an authority on his subject but an inexperienced writer. We are rigorously selective in the choice of books we publish. We set the highest standards of editorial quality and accuracy. This means that a *Paperfront* is easy to understand and delightful to read. Where illustrations are necessary to convey points of detail, these are drawn up by a subject specialist artist from our panel.

HOW WE KEEP PRICES LOW

We aim for the big seller. This enables us to order enormous print runs and achieve the lowest price for you. Unfortunately, this means that you will not find in the *Paperfront* list any titles on obscure subjects of minority interest only. These could not be printed in large enough quantities to be sold for the low price at which we offer this series. We sell almost all our *Paperfronts* at the same unit price. This saves a lot of fiddling about in our clerical departments and helps us to give you world-beating value. Under this system, the longer titles are offered at a price which we believe to be unmatched by any publisher in the world.

OUR DISTRIBUTION SYSTEM

Because of the competitive price, and the rapid turnover, *Paperfronts* are possibly the most profitable line a bookseller can handle. They are stocked by the best bookshops all over the world. It may be that your bookseller has run out of stock of a particular title. If so, he can order more from us at any time—we have a fine reputation for "same day" despatch, and we supply any order, however small (even a single copy), to any bookseller who has an account with us. We prefer you to buy from your bookseller, as this reminds him of the strong underlying public demand for *Paperfronts*. Members of the public who live in remote places, or who are housebound, or whose local bookseller is unco-operative, can order direct from us by post.

FREE

If you would like an up-to-date list of all paperfront titles currently available, send a stamped self-addressed envelope to
ELLIOT RIGHT WAY BOOKS, BRIGHTON RD.,
LOWER KINGSWOOD, SURREY, U.K.